Kiln Theatre in association with

SHANGHAI
by AMY NG
DOLLS

CAST

Lan Ping/Jiang Qing
Gabby Wong

Li Lin/Sun Weishi
Millicent Wong

CREATIVE TEAM

Playwright
Amy Ng

Director
Katie Posner

Designer
Jean Chan

Lighting Designer
Aideen Malone

Composer & Sound Designer
Nicola T. Chang

Video Designer
Akhila Krishnan

Movement Director
Annie-Lunnette Deakin-Foster

Associate Lighting Designer
Holly Ellis

Kiln-Mackintosh Resident Assistant Director
Imy Wyatt Corner

Costume Supervisor
Natalie Jackson

Wigs, Hair and Make-up Consultant
Jackie Saundercock

PRODUCTION TEAM

Production Manager
Charlotte Ranson

Company Stage Manager
Katie Bachtler

Deputy Stage Manager
Roni Neale

Assistant Stage Manager (Book Cover)
Rain An

Technician
Mae Elliott

Sound Technician
Tim Jan Eichelbaum

Wardrobe Manager
Sharon Bourke

Production Carpenter
Matt Day

Production Electrician
Paul Salmon

Production Sound Engineer
Matt Russell

Video Content
Georgia Clegg
Akhila Krishnan

Video System Designer & Engineer
Richard Wells

Video Programmer
Richard Wells
Stanley Orwin-Fraser

Lighting Programmer
Tamykha Patterson

Rigger
Jess Wilson

Set built by
Morrell and Bert

With thanks to
Vie J and Xi Qin
Windson Liong

CAST

GABBY WONG
LAN PING/JIANG QING

Theatre includes: *Pericles, Jew of Malta, Love's Sacrifice, Volpone, Troilus and Cressida* (RSC); *Macbeth, Othello* (Shakespeare's Globe); *Macbeth, The Winter's Tale* (National Theatre); *Maryland, Pah-La* (Royal Court Theatre); *Duchess of Malfi* (Citizens Theatre); *Life of Pi* (Crucible Theatre); *Doctor Faustus* (Jamie Lloyd Company); *Takeaway, Sinbad the Sailor* (Theatre Royal Stratford East); *One of Two Stories or Both* (Manchester International Festival); *Posh* – all female (Pleasance Theatre) and *The Last Days of Limehouse* (New Earth Theatre).

Television includes: *1899, KAOS* (Netflix); *EastEnders, Unprecedented* (BBC) and *Strangers* (ITV).

Film includes: *Rogue One, Indiana Jones and the Dial of Destiny*.

MILLICENT WONG
LI LIN/SUN WEISHI

Theatre credits include: *The Mosinee Project* (Edinburgh Fringe); *The Crucible* (Sheffield Crucible); *Sputnik Sweetheart* (Arcola Theatre); *Orlando* (Garrick Theatre); *Henry V* (Donmar Warehouse); *Athena* (Yard Theatre); *Afterlife* (National Theatre); *The Doctor* (Duke of York's Theatre); *The Lion, The Witch and The Wardrobe* (Bridge Theatre); *The King of Hell's Palace* (Hampstead Theatre); *Pah-La* (Royal Court Theatre); *Six Degrees of Separation, Macbeth, Richard III, A Streetcar Named Desire, A View from the Bridge, As You Like It, Closer, The Three Sisters* (Royal Central School of Speech and Drama); *Forbidden City: Portrait of an Empress* (Singapore Repertory Theatre) and *Beauty World* (Victoria Theatre, Singapore).

Television credits include: *The Undeclared War 2* (Channel 4); *Douglas is Cancelled* (ITV); *Dal Y Mellt* (Vox Pictures); *Silent Witness, Dracula* (BBC); and *Annika* (Alibi/UKTV).

Film credits include: *I Used To Be Famous*.

CREATIVE TEAM

AMY NG
PLAYWRIGHT

Amy Ng is a British-Hong Kong playwright. Her plays include: *Under the Umbrella* (Belgrade Theatre Coventry/UK Tour); *Acceptance* (Hampstead Theatre) and *Shangri-La* (Finborough Theatre). Radio plays include *Tiger Girls* (BBC Radio 4) and *Kilburn Passion* (BBC Radio 3). Adaptations include *Miss Julie* (Chester Storyhouse/UK Tour 2020, 2022/Singapore Repertory Theatre 2022, and a bilingual version for the Hong Kong International Arts Festival, 2024). Amy trained as a historian and is the author of '*Nationalism and Political Liberty*' (Oxford University Press). She is fluent in English, German and Chinese and regularly translates Chinese plays into English.

KATIE POSNER
DIRECTOR

For Kiln Theatre: *The Seven Ages of Patience*.

Katie Posner joined Paines Plough as Joint Artistic Director with Charlotte Bennett in August 2019. For Paines Plough, Katie has most recently directed: Fringe First award winning play *Strategic Love Play* by Miriam Battye; *You Bury Me* by Ahlam (Bristol Old Vic/Edinburgh Lyceum/The Orange Tree - winner of the Women's Prize for Playwriting); *You Bury Me* staged reading for the Edinburgh International Festival (Paines Plough/ Ellie Keel Productions/45 North); *Hungry* (Soho Theatre/Roundabout Edinburgh); *Really Big and Really Loud* (UK Tour) and *Black Love* (Co-Director for Roundabout - UK Tour).

Further productions as a director include: *Strategic Love Play* (Audible/Chase This Productions/ Minetta Lane Theatre, New York); *Richard, My Richard* (Shakespeare North

Playhouse/Theatre Royal Bury St Edmunds); *My Mother Said I Never Should* (Theatre by the Lake); *Mold Riots* (Theatr Clwyd); *Swallows & Amazons* (Storyhouse); *Babe* (Mercury Theatre); *Playing Up* (NYT); *Finding Nana* (New Perspectives); *Made in India* (Tamasha/Belgrade/ Pilot); *Everything is Possible: The York Suffragettes*, *End of Desire* (York Theatre Royal); *The Season Ticket* (Northern Stage); *A View from Islington North* (Out Of Joint); *In Fog and Falling Snow* (National Railway Museum); *Running on the Cracks* (Tron Theatre); *York Mystery Plays* (Museum Gardens York); *Blackbird, Ghost Town, Clocking In* and *A Restless Place* (Pilot Theatre).

JEAN CHAN
DESIGNER

For Kiln Theatre: *Reason You Should(n't) Love Me*, *The Darkest Part of the Night*.

Jean Chan studied at the Royal Welsh College of Music and Drama, graduating in 2008 with a BA Hons Degree in Theatre Design. She went on to work as a resident designer, part of the Royal Shakespeare Company's Trainee Design Programme 2008-09. In 2009 she won the Linbury Prize for Stage Design.

Theatre Design credit include: *Rise* (Bradford 2025, UK City of Culture); *Lost and Found* (Factory International, Manchester); *The Meaning of Zong* (Barbican/Bristol Old Vic); *Twelfth Night, A Midsummer Night's Dream* (Shakespeare's Globe); *Pinocchio, Garbage King* (Unicorn Theatre); *Open Mic* (ETT/Soho Theatre); *Wild Goose, Plastic* (Theatre Royal Bath); *This Girl Laughs This Girl Cries This Girl Does Nothing* (Stellar Quines); *Dick Whittington, Jack and the Beanstalk* (Lyric Hammersmith); *Ticking* (Trafalgar Studios); *The Witches*,

James and the Giant Peach, The BFG (Dundee Rep); Jumpy, Hedda Gabler (The Royal Lyceum, Edinburgh); The Season Ticket (Pilot Theatre/Northern Stage); Cyrano De Bergerac (The Royal & Derngate/Northern Stage); Petula, Mother Courage, Bordergames and Tonypandemonium (National Theatre Wales).

Costume Design credits include: Becoming Nancy (Birmingham Rep); Miss Saigon (Scenekvelder, Oslo); Legally Blonde (Regent's Park Open Air Theatre); Knights' Tale (Toho Theatre, Japan); The Grinning Man (Trafalgar Studios/Bristol Old Vic); Aladdin (Lyric Hammersmith) and Lionboy (Complicité).

Opera Designs Include: LaCalisto (Longborough Opera Festival).

Associate Design credits include: Les Liaisons Dangereuses (Theatre Cocoon, Japan); The James Plays (National Theatre Scotland and Great Britain); Lionboy (Complicite); Five Guys Named Moe (Underbelly/Theatre Royal Stratford East) and Monsters (Arcola Theatre).

AIDEEN MALONE
LIGHTING DESIGNER

Theatre credits include: Kyoto (RSC); Twelfth Night (Regent's Park Open Air Theatre); Dracula (National Theatre Scotland); Tess of the d'Ubervilles (Peacock Theatre); Lemons Lemons Lemons Lemons Lemons (Harold Pinter Theatre); You Bury Me (Bristol Old Vic); Duet for One (Orange Tree); The Clothes They Stood Up In (Nottingham Playhouse); Wonder Boy (Bristol Old Vic); Running With Lions (Lyric Hammersmith); Hamlet (Young Vic); Old Bridge (Bush Theatre); A Kind of People (Royal Court); Death of a Salesman (Young Vic/Piccadilly Theatre); A Monster Calls (Old Vic/Bristol Old Vic/Parco Japan); Brighton Rock (York Theatre Royal); La Strada (The Other Palace); Jane Eyre & Peter Pan (National Theatre/Bristol Old Vic); Hetty Feather (Duke of York) and A Raisin in the Sun (Sheffield Theatre).

Musical credits include: Fiddler on the Roof, Carousel (Regent's Park Open Air Theatre); Talent (Sheffield Theatre); Now is Good (Storyhouse) and The Worst Witch (Vaudeville Theatre).

Dance credits include: Outwitting the Devil and Kaash (Akram Kahn Co); Darbar Festival (Sadlers Wells); Unkindest Cut (Sadhana); Time Over Distance Over Time (Liz Roche) and La Tete (Jasmin Vardimon).

Opera credits include: Ariodante, Turn of the Screw, The Marriage of Figaro, A Midsummers Night's Dream, Mary Queen of Scots, Cosi Fan Tutte and Jenufa/Tosca (English Touring Opera).

Architectural credits include: Sadlers Wells East Foyer.

NICOLA T. CHANG 張彤
COMPOSER & SOUND DESIGNER

For Kiln Theatre: The Ballad of Hattie and James.

Nicola T. Chang is a composer/ sound designer for stage and screen. She was a co-winner of the Evening Standard Future Theatre Fund (Audio Design) in 2021, and has received a WhatsOnStage nomination for Best Sound Design, four Off West-End Award nominations in Sound Design and a BroadwayWorldUK nomination in both Sound Design and Musical Direction. She has performed with the Chineke! Orchestra, the Women of the World Orchestra and the London Film Music Orchestra, and at venues such as the Royal Albert Hall, the Royal Festival Hall and Shakespeare's Globe. Her works include the three Olivier-nominated plays: For Black Boys Who Have Considered Suicide When the Hue Gets Too Heavy, The Swell and A Playlist for the Revolution.

Theatre credits include: For Black Boys Who Have Considered Suicide When the Hue Gets Too Heavy (Garrick Theatre/Royal Court/New Diorama); My Neighbour Totoro, All Mirth and No Matter (RSC); The Importance of Being Earnest, Kerry Jackson (National Theatre); Skeleton Crew (Donmar Warehouse); Minority

Report (Nottingham Playhouse/ Birmingham Rep/Lyric Hammersmith); *Escaped Alone and What If If Only* (Manchester Royal Exchange); *White Pearl, Sound of the Underground* (Royal Court); *Tribe, Of the Cut* (Young Vic); *The Ministry of Lesbian Affairs* (Soho Theatre); *The Swell, Little Baby Jesus* (Orange Tree); *A Playlist for the Revolution* (Bush Theatre); *Feral Monster* (National Theatre Of Wales); *A Doll's House* (Sheffield Crucible); *Reverberation* (Bristol Old Vic); *Dziady* (Almeida Theatre) and *The Death of Ophelia* (Shakespeare's Globe).

As a performer, theatre credits include: *Fantastically Great Women Who Changed The World* (Assistant MD/Keys 2/Percussion – The Other Palace); *SIX* (Deputy MD/Keys 1 – Arts Theatre) and *STOMP* (Ambassadors Theatre/World Tour).

AKHILA KRISHNAN
VIDEO DESIGNER

Akhila Krishnan is an award-winning projection designer and creative director for moving image and immersive technology. She trained at the Royal College of Art and the National Institute of Design in India and was previously Senior Designer at 59 Productions.

Theatre credits include: *Hamlet* (RSC); *Kyoto* (@sohoplace/RSC); *Dr Strangelove* (Noel Coward Theatre/ Bordgais); *Grenfell: In the Words of Survivors* (National Theatre/St Ann's Warehouse, New York); *Withnail and I, Sinatra, What's New Pussycat* (Birmingham Rep); *Our Generation* (National Theatre/Chichester Festival Theatre); *Natasha, Pierre and the Great Comet of 1812* (Pittsburgh CLO); *Assassins* (Chichester Festival Theatre); *Mandela, Chasing Hares* (Young Vic); *Come Fall In Love – The DDLJ Musical* (Old Globe, San Diego); *The Two Character Play* (Hampstead Theatre); *Oliver Twist* (Leeds Playhouse/Ramps on the Moon); *While You are Here* (The Place/Dance East) and *Maggot Moon* (Unicorn Theatre).

Opera and Classical Music credits include: *The Handmaid's Tale, The Rhinegold, The Valkyrie* (English National Opera); *O Flower of Fire* (Staatsoper Hannover); *Die Meistersinger von Nurnberg* (Wiener Staatsoper); *The Wreckers* (Glyndebourne); *Samson et Dalila, The Knife of Dawn, Echoes at the Gate, 8bit* (Royal Opera House); *The Dreaming Species* (Fuel) and *Syllable* (Theatre O).

Live Broadcast and Film Direction credits include: *POD, Lifesongs* (Guildhall).

Event design credits include: *Sound of Colour: Arrivals* (Arthouse Jersey); *Die Gelbe Tapete* (Kunstlerstipendium NRW, Cologne); *Sound of Colour: Origins* (Arthouse Jersey); *Mamma Mia: The Party* (O2 Arena) and *UpNext* (National Theatre Fundraising Gala).

She is the Interdisciplinary Fellow at the RSC 2024-25.

ANNIE-LUNNETTE DEAKIN FOSTER
MOVEMENT DIRECTOR

Annie-Lunnette Deakin-Foster is a London based movement director and choreographer.

Theatre credits include: *Romeo and Juliet* (Belgrade Theatre/Bristol Old Vic/Hackney Empire); *Lavender, Hyacinth, Violet, Yew* (Bush Theatre); *Treasure Island* (Orange Tree); *Pericles* (RSC/Chicago Shakespeare Theatre); *A Midsummer Night's Dream* (RSC/ Barbican Theatre); *Richard, My Richard* (Shakespeare North); *Othello, A Midsummer Night's Dream* (Globe); *The Little Matchgirl and Happier Tales* (Wise Children/Shakespeare's Globe/UK Tour); *Sleeping Beauty, Robin Hood, Beauty and the Beast, The Panto That Nearly Never Was, Pavilion* (Theatr Clwyd); *The Famous Five* (Chichester Festival Theatre/ Theatr Clwyd); *Beautiful Thing* (Stratford East/Leeds Playhouse/ HOME Manchester); *The Tempest Re-imagined* (Regent's Park Open Air Theatre/Unicorn Theatre); *The*

Flood (Queen's Theatre); *You Bury Me* (Bristol Old Vic/UK tour); *Lemons Lemons Lemons Lemons Lemons* (Harold Pinter Theatre); *Heart* (Minetta Lane Theatre, New York); *Romeo & Juliet/Little Women* (Grosvenor Park Open Air Theatre); *An Octoroon* (Abbey Theatre); *Cock* (Ambassadors Theatre); *Mum* (Soho Theatre/Theatre Royal Plymouth); *Rockets and Blue Lights* (National Theatre); *Black Victorians* (National Theatre); *Overflow, Chiaroscuro* (Bush Theatre); *The Bee in Me, Aesop's Fables, Grimm Tales* (Unicorn Theatre); *You Stupid Darkness* (Southwark Playhouse); *The Last Noel* (Arts at the Old Fire Station/UK tour); *On The Other Hand We're Happy, Daughterhood, Dexter and Winters Detective Agency* (Roundabout); Pop Music (National Tour); *The Court Must Have a Queen* (Hampton Court Palace) and *The Little Prince* (Omnibus Theatre).

HOLLY ELLIS
ASSOCIATE LIGHTING DESIGNER

Holly Ellis is a graduate of LAMDA's technical theatre course.

Associate Lighting Design credits includes: *Kyoto* (@Sohoplace for Aideen Malone); *A Sherlock Carol* (Marylebone Theatre for Rui Rita) and *Jabala and the Jin* (Belgrade Theatre for Aideen Malone).

Lighting Designer credits include: *Personal Values* (Hampstead Theatre); *Double Act, I'm Gonna Marry You Tobey Maguire, Blanket Ban* (Southwark Playhouse); *Instructions for A Teenage Armageddon* – Offwestend Nomination for Best Lighting Design (Southwark Playhouse). *Bright Places, The Promise* (Birmingham Rep/UK Touring); *The Barber of Seville* (Waterperry Opera); *Errol's Garden* (UK Tour); *The Long Run* (New Diorama Theatre/UK Tour); *Spy for Spy* (Riverside Studios); *On the Ropes* (Park Theatre); *Casteing* (Roundabout) and *Animal Kingdom* (Hampstead Theatre Downstairs).

IMY WYATT CORNER
KILN-MACKINTOSH RESIDENT
ASSISTANT DIRECTOR

For Kiln: *The Purists, Pins and Needles, The Lonely Londoners.*

Imy Wyatt Corner is Resident Assistant Director at Kiln Theatre. She trained on the Drama Directing MA at Bristol Old Vic Theatre School.

Directing credits include: *The Last One* (Arcola Theatre); *Passing* (Park Theatre); *Scarlet Sunday* (Omnibus Theatre); *Duck* (Arcola Theatre); *BEASTS* (Edinburgh Fringe); *A Midsummer Night's Dream* (The Grove DIY Skatepark); *Humane* (Pleasance Theatre); *Walk Swiftly & with Purpose* (North Wall Arts Centre/Theatre503); *Baby, What Blessings* (Theatre503/ Bunker Theatre) and *Happy Yet?* (Edinburgh Fringe/International Theatre, Frankfurt).

Associate/Assistant Director credits include: *Private Lives* (Ambassadors Theatre); *Relatively Speaking* (Theatre Royal Bath/UK Tour); *The Dance of Death* (Theatre Royal Bath/UK Tour); *Love All* (Jermyn Street Theatre) and *The Straw Chair* (Finborough Theatre). She was a Creative Associate at Jermyn Street Theatre 2022/3 and an Associate Artist at Arcola Theatre 2023/4.

NATALIE JACKSON
COSTUME SUPERVISOR

Natalie is an Essex Based Set & Costume Designer working mostly between London and Essex. She is a graduate of the BA Theatre Practice: Design for stage Course at Royal Central School of Speech and Drama.

Theatre credits include: *DNA* (Queens Theatre, Hornchurch); *Boudica* (Clifftown Theatre, Southend); *Just Loose it* (The Space); *The Last Winter* (Purple Mountain Theatre, Nanjing); *The Last Five Years* (Buxton Opera House); *The Making of Ali and Nino* (South Hill Arts Centre) and *And then the Fall* (RCSSD).

K<small>THEATRE</small> L N

'Kiln Theatre has revitalised the cultural life of Brent and brings world-class theatre at an affordable price to people from all walks of life.' **Zadie Smith**

Kiln Theatre sits in the heart of Kilburn in Brent, a unique and culturally diverse area of London where over 140 languages are spoken. We are a welcoming and proudly local venue, with an internationally acclaimed programme of world and UK premieres. Our work presents the world through a variety of lenses, amplifying unheard/ignored voices into the mainstream, exploring and examining the threads of human connection that cross race, culture and identity.

'This place was a special cocoon. Now she has grown and blossomed into a beautiful butterfly.' **Sharon D Clarke**

We believe that theatre is for all and want everyone to feel welcome and entitled to call the Kiln their own. We are committed to nurturing the talent of young people and local communities, to provide a platform for their voices to be heard.

'I wanted to say thank you for creating the most diverse theatre I have been to. In terms of race, culture, class, age, everything – not only in the selection of shows and actors, but in the audience.' **Audience member**

Kiln Theatre, 269 Kilburn High Road, London, NW6 7JR

KilnTheatre.com | info@KilnTheatre.com

 @KilnTheatre

Supported by
ARTS COUNCIL ENGLAND

Registration No. 1396429.
Registered Charity No. 276892

Paines Plough

Hello! We're Paines Plough, a theatre company led by Joint Artistic Directors Charlotte Bennett and Katie Posner. Dedicated entirely to new writing, we discover, develop and empower writers and share their stories with audiences all over the UK and beyond.

Founded in 1974, we have worked with over 500 playwrights including James Graham, Sarah Kane, Nathan Bryon, Abi Morgan, Kae Tempest, Vinay Patel, Mike Bartlett, Chloe Moss, Dennis Kelly, Zia Ahmed and Anna Jordan. Our plays are nationally discovered and locally heard. Each year, we tour our shows to over 30,000 people and work with 400 writers across the country through our multi-year writer development programme, Tour The Writer.

'An essential part of the UK's new writing ecology... its nationwide place in that has only grown in recent years.' **Lyn Gardner, Stage Door**

In 2019, alongside Ellie Keel, we co-founded the Women's Prize for Playwriting to redress the gender imbalance of the stories being told on our national stages, and we have co-produced and toured two of the winners so far: *Reasons You Should(n't) Love Me* by Amy Trigg and *You Bury Me* by Ahlam, with 2022 winner *Consumed* by Karis Kelly set to tour in 2025.

'The lifeblood of the UK's theatre ecosystem.' **Guardian**

Joint Artistic Directors & CEOs | **Charlotte Bennett** & **Katie Posner**
Executive Director | **Jodie Gilliam**
Producer | **Ellie Fitz-Gerald**
Marketing & Audience Development Manager | **Manwah Siu**
Administrator | **Hannah Churchill**
Press Representative | **Bread and Butter PR**

Board of Directors | **Ankur Bahl, Corey Campbell, Lauren Dark, Asma Hussain, Helen Perryer, Farha Quadri, Carolyn Saunders, Kully Thiarai (Chair)**

office@painesplough.com www.painesplough.com
Follow us on Instagram, Bluesky, Facebook, YouTube and LinkedIn. Donate to Paines Plough at justgiving.com/PainesPlough Paines Plough Limited is a company limited by guarantee and a registered charity. Registered Company no: 1165130. Registered Charity no: 267523 Paines Plough, c/o Belgrade Theatre, Belgrade Square, Corporation Street, Coventry CV1 1GS. London office: 38 Mayton Street, N7 6QR

Supported using public funding by
ARTS COUNCIL ENGLAND
LOTTERY FUNDED

CREATIVE ENGAGEMENT AT KILN THEATRE

We create projects with and for people of all ages who live, learn or work in Brent and North West London. Our programmes encourage people to have fun, connect, be creative, discover a career or an interest in theatre and have their voices heard.

LEARNING

We believe all young people should have access to arts and culture, and experience the wider benefits the arts can have on connection and confidence. Arrive Build Create (formerly Minding the Gap) has been running for 18 years, working with EAL and ESOL departments in local schools and colleges to provide creative drama based sessions for newly arrived young people. The project aims to develop creativity, confidence and engagement in the arts. We also have opportunities for participants to develop their skills further through the Arrive Build Create Trainees programme and the Young Company. We provide resources and training for teachers working with EAL/ESOL students. For Brent schools, we run free Backstage Workshops, Continuous Professional Development for teachers, School Residencies; a bespoke year-long programme designed with local schools to support the Drama curriculum and link to the industry. We also host Teacher Previews and provide free Resource Packs. We deliver Fullworks; a weeklong half term project which explores careers in theatre, open to students from Brent schools aged 14-16 and Placements (in partnership with Further and Higher Education centres).

PARTICIPATION

Our Participation work is rooted in Brent & North West London and celebrates the unique cultural and artistic life of our local area. The Participation programme covers all work with and for local residents who are interested in engaging in theatre as aspiring artists or audiences, providing opportunities to have fun and socialise, or share stories with neighbours. We aim to listen to and advocate for the priorities, heritages and stories of local residents through co-creation. We run a Youth Theatre for 12-15 and 16-18 year olds, nurturing the next generation of artists. We host Dementia Friendly film screenings each month and Kiln Masterclasses every quarter, delivered by creatives from Kiln shows. From 2024-26 we're embarking on an ambitious community engaged heritage project. Celebrating Our Stories: the Kilburn High Road Project, celebrates and platforms the hidden stories of the High Road and the residents, artists, businesses and organisations who call Kilburn home. This project is made possible with The National Lottery Heritage Fund with thanks to National Lottery Players. For more information on how to get involved with this project, please visit our website.

For more information about our work and how to get involved, see our website **kilntheatre.com/ creative-engagement**, email us on **getinvolved@kilntheatre.com** or scan the QR code.

SUPPORT OUR WORK

Kiln Theatre is a proudly local theatre with a world-class reputation. We create bold and engaging work which amplifies unheard voices. Every year, we must raise close to £1 million in order to stage extraordinary theatre, inspire the next generation of artists, and keep our doors open and our lights on. Will you help us?

BECOME A KILN FRIEND

From just £5 per month, you can enjoy:

- Access to Priority Booking
- Exclusive updates and insights from Kiln
- Invitations to special supporters' events

You can also become a Kiln Friend at Silver or Gold level, which offers an even wider range of exciting opportunities.

KILN CIRCLE

The Kiln Circle is a supporters' group that sits at the heart of our theatre. The Circle are given special opportunities to get close to the work on our stage and the artists involved in each of our productions, alongside invitations to exclusive events and Press Nights. Donations start from £2,500 per year.

SECURE THE FUTURE OF KILN THEATRE

Could you invest in the future of Kiln Theatre by leaving a gift to us in your will?

By leaving a gift in your will - no matter the size - you will help to ensure that Kiln remains a place where stories are told, creativity flourishes and everyone is welcomed. To inform us of your plans, or to discuss how you can make a difference through a gift in your will, please contact the Fundraising Team using the details below. All conversations will be handled with discretion and care.

HOW TO DONATE

To join our community of supporters today, scan the QR code, visit KilnTheatre.com/give or call Catherine and Alannah on 020 7625 0132.

Supported by
ARTS COUNCIL ENGLAND

Registration No. 1396429.
Registered Charity No. 276892

A BIG THANK YOU TO ALL OUR SUPPORTERS

We would not be able to continue our work without the support of the following:

STATUTORY FUNDERS

Arts Council England
Brent Council Warm Spaces
Camden Council Learning Support Fund
The National Lottery Heritage Fund

COMPANIES

The Agency (London) Ltd
Breathe HR
JPC Law

MAJOR DONORS AND KILN CIRCLE

Nick and Aleksandra Barnes
The Basden Family
Primrose and David Bell
Torrence Boone
Jules and Cheryl Burns
Mary and Jim Callaghan
Chalmers Family Foundation
Laure Zanchi Duvoisin
Gary and Carol Fethke
Matthew Greenburgh and Helen Payne
Ros and Alan Haigh
Mary Clancy Hatch
Melanie J. Johnson
Linda Keenan
Claire-Bridget Kenwright
Jonathan Levy and Gabrielle Rifkind
Brian and Clare Linden
Frances Magee
Dame Susie Sainsbury
Jon and NoraLee Sedmak
Jan and Michael Topham

INDIVIDUALS AND LEGACIES

M. Michele Burns and Deborah A. Jamison
Ian Chalmers
Henry Chu and James Baer
John and Susan Coldstream
Maria de Esteban Belzuz
Sue Fletcher
Gillian Hooper
Nicola Horton and Tiffany Evans
Nazima Kadir and Karl Gorz
Frances Lynn
Sita McIntosh
Alison McLean and Michael Farthing
Harry Frank Rose
Ann and Peter Sprinz
Emma Thompson and Greg Wise

TRUSTS AND FOUNDATIONS

29th May 1961 Charitable Trust
The Atkin Foundation
Backstage Trust
Bertha Foundation
Boris Karloff Charitable Foundation
Christina Smith Foundation
City Bridge Foundation - London's biggest independent charity funder
The John S Cohen Foundation
The D'Oyly Carte Charitable Trust
Esmée Fairbairn Foundation
The Foyle Foundation
John Lyon's Charity
The Mackintosh Foundation
Maria Björnson Memorial Fund
Marie-Louise von Motesiczky Charitable Trust
Pears Foundation
Richard Radcliffe Trust
The Roddick Foundation
Royal Victoria Hall Foundation
Stanley Thomas Johnson Foundation
Theatre Artists Fund Pilot Programme
Three Monkies Trust
The Vanderbilt Family Foundation
The Vandervell Foundation

And all those who wish to remain anonymous.

FOR KILN THEATRE

SHANGHAI DOLLS

Amy Ng

Characters

LAN PING/JIANG QING (1914–1991), *actress who married Mao Zedong and started the Cultural Revolution. Twenty-one years old at the start of the play.*

LI LIN/SUN WEISHI (1921–1968), *the first woman director in China. Daughter of a Communist martyr, later adopted by Mao's number two, Premier Zhou Enlai. Fourteen years old at the start of the play.*

Notes on the Text

A forward slash (/) indicate overlapping text.

An em-dash (—) indicates a hard or loaded silence.

This text went to press before the end of rehearsals and so may differ slightly from the play as performed.

News

Projections of headlines (the Chinese ones are subtitled in English):

'Shanghai Times, *June 1935: 20 Communist Terrorists Executed in Shanghai.*'

'Red China, *June 1935: Kuomintang cedes control of North China to Japanese army.*'

'China Critic, *June 1935: Open Auditions Announced for Upcoming Production of* A Doll's House.'

A red pen circles this last item of news.

Lights up on LAN PING, *as she reads the newspapers, pen in hand.*

Scene One

Titles: 'Shanghai, 1935.'

A rehearsal room.

LAN PING *warms up vocally with Ibsen's lines.*

The sound of knocking.

LAN PING *tries to ignore the knocking.*

LI LIN, *fourteen, enters. She's dressed in a shapeless black dress, her possessions in a large cloth bundle, clutching a rag doll.*

LAN PING   'I must make up my mind who is right – the world or I.'

LI LIN	I'm sorry?
LAN PING	'I believe that I am first and foremost a human being.'
LI LIN	Of course you're human.
LAN PING	Even if you hadn't *bothered* to read the script, you should at least *recognise* Nora's iconic lines.
LI LIN	Who's Nora?
LAN PING	I suppose you are a bit young for *A Doll's House*.
LI LIN	(*Looking around*.) What doll's house?
LAN PING	The funeral parlour's next door.
LI LIN	(*Getting upset*.) Who died?
LAN PING	How would I know? Shanghai's a big city.
LI LIN	But why did you tell me the funeral parlour's next door?
LAN PING	(*Slow and distinct*.) Because. The. Funeral. Parlour. Is. Next. Door.
LI LIN	Is this a code? (*Hopefully*.) A message? From my mother?
LAN PING	No one asked me to pass on no message, okay? Now if you don't mind I need to focus.
LI LIN	Then why did you bring up the funeral parlour?
LAN PING	You're in black. You've never heard of *A Doll's House*. You can't possibly be here for auditions –
LI LIN	Auditions? (*Scandalised*.) You're an actress.
LAN PING	(*Spooky voice*.) Yes. I'm an actress. Boo.
LI LIN	I have nothing against actresses.
LAN PING	I'll have you know, this isn't some disreputable semi-brothel of a touring opera. This is the home of modern theatre. Of dangerous plays. That will

blow up the System. This is a home for arsonists. I'm an arsonist. Are you?

A thoroughly intimidated LI LIN *backs away to a far corner. Consults a piece of paper.*

LI LIN   This is… 780 Consulate Road?

LAN PING   Yes.

LI LIN   Is it… just a theatre?

LAN PING   It's the headquarters of the League of Left-Wing Dramatists.

LI LIN   (*Gloriously relieved.*) The Left-Wing League! (*Softer.*) A safe house.

LAN PING   Safe rooms are in the attic.

LI LIN   Is Mummy here? Is *Papa Zhou* here?

LAN PING   Sugar-daddy?

LI LIN   (*Uncomprehending.*) My father's sworn brother. He's looked out for us since Father's death.

LAN PING   Taking your dead daddy's place in your mummy's bed?

LI LIN   No! How dare you!

            LAN PING *smirks.*

LAN PING   No one's there.

            LI LIN *sinks down in the corner, shuddering. She hugs her rag doll.*

            (*Nicer.*) Have you eaten?

            LI LIN *shakes her head.*

            Here. Have a macaroon.

            LAN PING *carefully takes out a box of macaroons from her bag, and hands one to* LI LIN. LI LIN *wolfs it down.*

LI LIN   It's delicious.

LAN PING   From the Kiessling café in the French
              Concession. Hideously expensive. But so good.

              LAN PING *snaps the box shut.*

              LI LIN *looks crestfallen.*

              Oh go on then.

              LAN PING *opens the box again.*

              LI LIN *eagerly takes another.*

              You look like you haven't eaten in a week.

              LI LIN *tears up.*

              You really haven't eaten in a week. Who's taking
              care of you?

LI LIN   The Party takes care of me.

LAN PING   Not doing a very good job then, are they?

LI LIN   They do too! They came at dawn, banged on my
              door, told me there would be a raid and I was to
              come here and make myself useful. (*Fretfully.*)
              Mummy would be furious if she knew they'd sent
              me to a theatre.

LAN PING   You'd better be off then.

LI LIN   The Party sent me here.

LAN PING   (*Mocking salute.*) Obey the Party. Obey the Party.
              Good little cadres obey the Party.

LI LIN   You're not a Communist?

LAN PING   Of course I'm a Communist.

LI LIN   How can you be so disrespectful so –

LAN PING   An obedient revolutionary? Oxymoron, no?

LI LIN   Oh.

              Pause. LI LIN *considers this novel point of view.*
              She eats another macaroon.

LAN PING   Hey hey hey. I need them to get into character. Nora's always sneaking macaroons behind her husband's back.

LI LIN   Sorry.

            Beat.

            Why does Nora have to sneak macaroons?

LAN PING   You really don't know anything? I'll show you. Wait there.

            LAN PING *exits, then re-enters dramatically.*

            Nora enters in her fur coat – beautiful, young, in love – carrying Christmas presents. She lays out the presents under the tree. She crams macaroons into her mouth. Her husband Torvald calls from off-stage 'Is that you, my little skylark!' Nora swallows quickly and hides the macaroons.

LI LIN   (*Engrossed.*) And then?

LAN PING   Well, this elegant, cosy, rich Western world turns out to be very much like ours. Women aren't allowed to sign cheques or borrow money. But Nora has borrowed money... When her husband fell sick and she needed money to save him, she took out a loan from a certain Krogstad, forging her father's signature on the bond, then working herself to the bone to repay her debt. Krogstad blackmails her anyway – your past always catches up with you...

LI LIN   Then what?

LAN PING   Torvald finds out. He's furious, worried sick, not about her going to jail for forgery, but about his reputation. Nora realises her life is built on a lie. That her noble husband is in fact a coward. That he doesn't see her as a human being, but a human doll. So she walks out of his home and slams the door shut.

            Pause.

LI LIN   What happens after Nora leaves home?

LAN PING   She's going to go hungry. She's going to sleep
                rough. She'll have to walk dark streets at night.
                Which makes me the perfect Nora. I ask you,
                who would you choose to play Nora? A refined
                young lady – what would she know of the world
                outside? She'd come crawling back to her Torvald
                within the week. Whereas my Nora would choose
                to leave, in full consciousness of what that
                means – starvation, disgrace, maybe even death.
                Who deserves the role huh?

LI LIN   You do. And I'm sure you'll get it.

LAN PING   Why?

LI LIN   You painted pictures in my head.

LAN PING   (*Eagerly.*) Did I really? (*Despondent.*) I won't get
                it.

LI LIN   You sound the part.

LAN PING   I spent years polishing my accent. Some rich
                actress will get it.

LI LIN   But this is the Left-Wing League –

LAN PING   – of Champagne Communists.

LI LIN   (*With conviction.*) Your talent will blaze out.

LAN PING   (*Quietly.*) Thank you. What's your name?

LI LIN   Li Lin.

LAN PING   What a plain name.

LI LIN   I don't want to stand out.

LAN PING   How are you going to get anywhere in life
                without standing out? We'll have to come up with
                a new name for you –

LI LIN   They're cracking down again. They're shooting
                Party members. We'll be killed if we 'stand out'!
                How do I get to the safe rooms?

LAN PING   Stop right there. The Party told you to make
            yourself useful. Help me with this last scene.
            (*Handing her the script*.) You read the husband's
            lines. From here.

            LAN PING *hands* LI LIN *a script*.

            During the following excerpt, LAN PING *plays
            Nora angry and hectoring*.

LI LIN   'May I write to you, Nora?'

LAN PING   'No, never.'

LI LIN   'I must send you – '

LAN PING   'Nothing.'

LI LIN   'I must help you – '

LAN PING   'I take nothing from strangers.'

LI LIN   'Nora, can I never be more than a stranger to
            you?'

LAN PING   'Oh Torvald, then the miracle of miracles would
            have to happen.'

            LI LIN *puts down the script*.

LI LIN   What is the miracle of miracles?

LAN PING   That men can actually change. But that's
            impossible. That's why she's so angry.

LI LIN   (*Beat*.) I think she's more pained than angry. You
            know when you're little and you think there is
            actual magic in the world...

LAN PING   You mean, like when you're walking alone on
            dark streets and you're terrified of zombies?

LI LIN   No no, the good magic. Daddy loved Christmas.
            He made us clean our shoes and put them out for
            St Nicholas –

LAN PING   Who's St Nicholas?

LI LIN   Tall, very tall; red and white robes, gives presents
                to good children. In the morning our shoes would
                be stuffed to the big toe with chestnuts, a spinning
                top, a few coins… The Christmas after Daddy
                died, we put out our shoes for St Nicholas. But in
                the morning the shoes were empty. (*Beat*.) I think
                that is Nora's pain.

                Pause.

                'Nora, can I never be more than a stranger to
                you?'

LAN PING   (*Melodramatically pained*.) 'Oh Torvald, then the
                miracle of miracles would have to happen.'

                LI LIN *flinches*.

                (*Defensively*.) What? Too melodramatic?

LI LIN   …Noisy. She's listening for a sign. She doesn't
                want to take this step. She wants them to…
                choose… a different world.

                Beat.

LAN PING   I've had so many directors bang on about the
                emotional undercurrent beneath the text. You're
                the only one who's ever plugged me into that
                current. Li Lin, you were born to be a director.
                The first woman theatre director in China.

LI LIN   Oh no no. I'm going to… Mummy says – I've got
                to go upstairs.

LAN PING   I wouldn't…
                They raided the safe rooms this morning.

LI LIN   (*Panicked*.) What do we do now?

LAN PING   Keep calm and run lines.

LI LIN   At a time like this?!

LAN PING   (*Hard*.) Especially at a time like this. We go to
                the theatre like we go to the temple. The world

outside may be going to hell in a handbasket,
but here, in the theatre, that other world of truth,
beauty, justice is so close, we can almost reach
out and touch it.

LI LIN   I have to find another safe house. Mummy must –

LAN PING   There are no more safe houses. They've smashed
the Shanghai Party organisation. Come stay with
me!

LI LIN   Are you crazy? The Central Committee –

LAN PING   Is far away. Nothing is safe. Come on. It'll be
fun! This is fate, Li Lin. Of all the theatres in all
the towns in all of China, you had to walk into
this one. It will be us against the world.

LI LIN   Okay.

*LAN PING takes off her scarf, drapes it around
LI LIN, then knots it artfully to create shape for
her dress.*

LAN PING   In twenty minutes a dozen young ladies will come
through this door to audition. Who are dressed by
Shanghai's most fashionable tailors. Who play
at revolution like they play tennis, but who can't
accept that the likes of you and me belong here.
Can't let the side down, can we?

LI LIN looks at her own reflection in the mirror.

She takes the script from LAN PING.

LI LIN   (*Commandingly.*) From the top.

'Nora, can I never be more than a stranger to
you?'

LAN PING   (*Anguished but restrained.*) 'Oh Torvald, then the
miracle of miracles would have to happen.'

LI LIN   'What is the miracle of miracles?'

LAN PING   'Both of us would have to change so that – oh
            Torvald, I no longer believe in miracles.'

LI LIN   'But I will believe. We must so change that – '

            LAN PING *takes* LI LIN*'s hand.*

LAN PING   (*Softly.*) 'That communion between us shall be
            a marriage.'

            LAN PING *turns around to face the audience.*
            She bows.

            Thunderous applause.

            Bouquets of flowers thrown at the stage.

            News:

            'China Critic: *1935 – the Year of Nora. The Year*
            of Lan Ping.'

Scene Two

Titles: 'Shanghai, 1936.'

The proverbial bohemian artist garret. Peeling wall paint,
a bare light bulb, a radio, a vase of roses on the rickety table.
A large poster of Lan Ping as Nora is tacked up on the wall.

LI LIN *packs her meagre possessions into a cloth bag. She*
hesitates, then leaves a letter for Lan Ping on their bed.

LI LIN *puts her rag doll into her bag. Then she takes it out*
again. She lays it next to Lan Ping's doll on her side of the bed.

The sound of footsteps running up stairs.

LI LIN   (*Flustered.*) Lan Ping! You're back early.

            The door is flung open, and LAN PING *enters*
            with shopping bags from luxury stores.

            (*Wryly.*) 'Nora enters, with bags of shopping.'

LAN PING   (*Snaps*.) Oh live dangerously, Li Lin!

LI LIN   You can't keep blowing the kitty on macaroons, then live off rice and soya sauce for weeks. No wonder your digestion –

LAN PING   Earn some proper money with a proper acting job if you're so worried, instead of faffing around with bullshit backstage gigs.

LI LIN   Mummy told me to keep a low profile.

LAN PING   We've been through this. Mummy's jealous of you.

LI LIN   And I'm not freeloading off you. I've been paying you rent this entire year – out of my understudy gigs.

LAN PING   Stick with me. You'll get the money back tenfold. This is an investment. In our future.

LAN PING *retrieves books.*

(*Enticingly*.) Chekhov… Gorky… Stanislavski *An Actor Prepares* – our Bible, Li Lin!

LI LIN *leaves through the books reverently.*

LI LIN   Lan Ping! The newest translation, with Chekhov's letters to Stanislavski… (*Yearning*.) 'To Moscow, to Moscow. Soon. Now.' Some day we'll get to the Moscow Arts Theatre!

LAN PING *takes out a silk qipao from her shopping.*

LAN PING   Aha! Isn't this gorgeous?

LI LIN   (*Shocked*.) How much did this cost?

LAN PING   It's an investment. (*Overtly casual*.) Tang Na is writing a profile on me.

LI LIN   The critic? That's huge!

LAN PING   He needs to feel I'm granting him a favour. I need him to see me as magnificent.

LI LIN   You are magnificent. You don't need to blow all
                your money on a dress –

LAN PING   Stop bellyaching, Li Lin. I've had a bit of a
                windfall. Look.

                LI LIN *takes out a rolled-up poster and unfurls it,*
                to reveal a portrait of Lan Ping coyly holding up
                a glass of Coke. She pins it up next to the poster
                of her as Nora.

LI LIN   (*Shocked.*) You're advertising Coca-Cola?

LAN PING   Two hundred dollars they paid me to hold up a
                glass of Coke.

LI LIN   That's… that's… capitalism!

LAN PING   It's only capitalism if the worker does not reap
                the fruit of their labours. I've reaped. Why
                shouldn't I? I never had no daddy stuff my shoe
                with silver coins.

                LI LIN *flinches, but holds her ground.*

LI LIN   It's the opiate of the people!

LAN PING   Coke?

LI LIN   What it represents! We are on the very brink
                of war, but the imperialists hypnotise us with
                consumerism –

LAN PING   Stop parroting the Party line. War war war. It's
                just their way of terrorising us into submission –

LI LIN   So the Japanese occupation of Manchuria is just
                fiction?

LAN PING   That's thousands of miles away. Shanghai's not
                going to fall.
                I'm going dancing with Tang Na. At the Black
                Cat cabaret in the Paris Hotel, tonight.

LI LIN   Are you and Tang Na…

LAN PING	Come along! (*Suggestively*.) Jin Shan's going to be there. Li Lin! You're blushing. Still waters run deep!
LI LIN	I'm not... I don't...
LAN PING	Oh come on. Who doesn't have a crush on Jin Shan? 'China's Clark Gable.'
LI LIN	He's much better looking than Clark Gable.
LAN PING	Oh oh this is serious. Where's that gorgeous kingfisher-blue dress I got you that you've never worn?

LAN PING *heads for the wardrobe which* LI LIN *has emptied.* LI LIN *blocks her.*

LI LIN	I can't go!
LAN PING	Your dance card's full tonight? Anyone I know?
LI LIN	I can't dance.
LAN PING	You couldn't act either. So you thought.

LAN PING *takes hold of* LI LIN *and shows her how to jitterbug. A shy* LI LIN *copies her, and eventually gets it.*

That's right. Whip him into a frenzy. Then when the slow dance comes around, move in for the kill...

LAN PING *demonstrates on* LI LIN, *grinding into her.*

LI LIN	Lan Ping, stop. Stop! I'm not... free and easy like you!

LAN PING *pats* LI LIN *down, searching for something.*

LAN PING	Aha...
LI LIN	Lan Ping!

LAN PING *finds a letter in* LI LIN's *pocket.*

LAN PING   I knew it. You're always so snarky when Mummy
            sends you a letter.

            LI LIN *tries to snatch back the letter.* LAN PING
            dances out of reach

LI LIN   Don't! She just found out we're living together.
            She's furious –

LAN PING   (*Reading.*) '…leave that notorious actress
            right away.' Notorious. Depraved. Debauched.
            Degenerate.

LI LIN   Her words.

LAN PING   Mummy's one of those Brides of the Party, isn't
            she? Puritanical. Pinched. Joyless.

LI LIN   She wasn't – Daddy and Papa Zhou used to take
            her out dancing –

LAN PING   Read Alexandra Kollontai – Soviet feminist,
            first woman ambassador *ever*: 'Free love equals
            revolution equals communism'! (*Beat.*) I could
            have been a rich man's mistress and never worry
            about work again. But am I? Have I ever sold
            myself for a role? You think I wanted to go from
            Nora to Coca-Cola? What happens to Nora after
            she leaves home? Does she have to sell her art,
            her body, her obedience – to survive?

LI LIN   In the socialist utopia Nora will be free and
            happy –

LAN PING   Artists need freedom. Free women are
            demonised. It is literally impossible to be
            a woman artist.

LI LIN   In Yan'an Nora will be free and happy and safe.

LAN PING   (*Reading from the letter*.) 'Leave for Yan'an
            today.'

LI LIN   (*Overly bright*.) Chairman Mao's base! Come
            with me! Mummy says they're building a new
            Soviet society there.

LAN PING   Oh please. Mao's troops had their arses kicked.
            They hid out in the caves and called it a Soviet.
            As far as I know, the Neanderthals never had no
            theatre.

LI LIN   And you call yourself a Communist!

LAN PING   What would I do in Yan'an? Hoe the soil? Plow
            the fields?

LI LIN   Make revolutionary theatre.

LAN PING   I joined a so-called revolutionary theatre troupe.
            We took 'plays' out to factories and street corners.
            When I say 'plays'... they were more like pulp
            after the Party censors had chewed them over.
            And then I was arrested for that shit.

LI LIN   (*Shocked*.) You went to jail?

LAN PING   Don't worry. I was fine. Jail gave me time to
            think: maybe we had committed a crime. A crime
            against art... Playing Nora was the first time
            I could be a true artist. That silence... when you
            strike the tuning fork, *when you hit the truth*, and
            suddenly those coughing, shuffling, chattering
            punters become one, like a symphony orchestra...

LI LIN   (*In a reverie, slowly*.) I know exactly what you
            mean.

LAN PING   You won't find that in Yan'an. Shanghai may be
            a crazy bitch city, but it's our crazy bitch city.
            You're staying put.

LI LIN   Lan Ping, I –

            The sound of temple bells.

LAN PING   Fuck! I'm late... You – feudal bells!

            LAN PING *slips into the elaborate qipao. She
            poses.*

            How do I look?

LI LIN   Gorgeous.

                LAN PING *looks at herself in the mirror.*
                Gradually a look of horror.

LAN PING   No no no. It's too gaudy. I look cheap.

LI LIN   Lan Ping, you are not cheap.

                LAN PING *feverishly rummages through her*
                wardrobe.

LAN PING   (*Determined.*) I'll make him respect me.

                LAN PING *puts on a pair of thick black-rimmed*
                glasses. It looks incongruous with the qipao.
                LI LIN *bursts out laughing.*

                (*Fiercely.*) Brains and beauty.

LI LIN   (*Realising.*) You're serious about him.

LAN PING   He completely agrees that an actress ain't no
                doll to be pushed around, but an artist in her own
                right!

LI LIN   (*Quietly.*) You'll leave me...

LAN PING   No! (*Beat.*) But with Tang Na at my side, the
                world will have to take me seriously.

LI LIN   You don't need me then –

LAN PING   I don't want to be the notorious Lan Ping. I want
                the world to see that I'm a revolutionary artist,
                with principles, and courage, and grit; who will
                never stop working to master my craft; never stop
                fighting to birth a new world!

                LI LIN *stands up, puts on her coat and picks up*
                her travel bag.

                Where are you going?

                So you choose Mummy over –

LI LIN   Not everything is about you! Mummy's afraid I'll
                be arrested –

LAN PING   What sort of revolutionary is she, worrying about arrest all the time!

LI LIN   My father was executed in jail.

Beat.

LAN PING   You didn't tell me that.

LI LIN   (*Softly.*) I wasn't supposed to.

LAN PING   (*Hard.*) And would a daughter of a revolutionary martyr run off to safety in Yan'an or stay on the frontline? You were sent by the Party to the theatre. You can't just abandon your post.

LI LIN   Why do you want me to stay in Shanghai? Just so you can leave me for Tang Na?

LAN PING   You're right. It's not all about me. What do you want?

LAN PING suddenly sets fire to the letter.

LI LIN   What are you doing?

LAN PING puts the burning letter on an ashtray in front of the Nora poster – the effect is that of incense sticks on an altar.

She links arms with LI LIN and pulls them both down into a kneeling position.

LAN PING   We, Lan Ping and...

LI LIN   Li Lin.

LAN PING   ...have come together today as sisters, to make revolution through theatre and to save women from men. Although we were not born in the same year the...

LI LIN   ...same month...

LAN PING   ...the same day or the same hour, we hope...

LI LIN   ...to die on the same year the same month the same day and the same hour.

LAN PING   May Marx and Lenin,

LI LIN   Chekhov and Ibsen,

LAN PING   witness to what is in our hearts.

LI/LAN   If we should ever do anything to betray our
            friendship, may Heaven and Earth strike us dead.

            They bow eight times.

News

'Shanghai Times, *7 July 1937: Fierce Fighting Breaks Out
between Japanese and Chinese Troops at the Marco Polo
Bridge, Beijing.'*

'Shanghai Times, *31 July 1937: Japanese Troops Take the
Marco Polo Bridge and Advance South.'*

Scene Three

Titles: 'Shanghai, 1937.'

A dressing room in a theatre during a performance.

LI LIN *enters, dressed in armour as Joan of Arc.*

The sound of knocking.

LI LIN   Who's there?

            LAN PING *enters, in a tuxedo and bowler hat,
            her face obscured by a large bouquet of roses.*

            (*Shrill.*) Members of the public can't come in
            here!

I said –

LAN PING *thrusts the bouquet at* LI LIN, *revealing herself.*

LAN PING   Congratulations!

LI LIN   (*Coldly.*) It's you.

LAN PING   Big star now. My little Li Lin.

LI LIN   I'm not a star.

LAN PING   Nonsense. That silence in the auditorium –

LI LIN   My housemate vanished, leaving three months' unpaid rent and ten dress invoices. How else was I meant to pay that off?

LAN PING   I'll pay you back /

LI LIN   / I thought you'd been run over, or arrested, or something. Then I read in the tabloids that you'd married Tang Na.

LAN PING   It wasn't like that! It was meant to be a holiday!

LI LIN   You mean a honeymoon –

LAN PING   I was swept off my feet...

Beat.

I'm sorry... But for once, why shouldn't I live like the other half?

LI LIN   So you married into the other half.

LAN PING   No!

Beat.

We only pretended to get married so his family would give him his inheritance.

LI LIN   Convenient –

LAN PING   But then he started acting as if we were back in imperial times, when a wife couldn't leave her husband's home –

LI LIN   Did soldiers stand guard at the door then?

LAN PING   He took my diaries. I was so worried he'd publish them or something.

LI LIN   I stuck with you, Lan Ping! You didn't stick with me! I waited in our home so you could find me. Then I realised you weren't coming back /

LAN PING   But / I'm here now! I would have come earlier but every time he ran after me, threatening to kill himself / if I left –

LI LIN   It's too late! / The road to Yan'an is blocked; the Japanese are twenty miles / away

LAN PING   I called / his bluff. I left last night. I took the train to Shanghai, and I saw your name in lights! You were born to rule the stage, Li Lin; it was worth something if my leaving forced you to take the plunge /

LI LIN   How dare / you

LAN PING   I / loved your Joan of Arc, Li Lin. The Party wants their women young, naive, stupid. The concubine died for the emperor. The modern woman dies for her country's honour. But you're giving them the wavering Joan of Arc, the weak Joan of Arc, you / clever girl

LI LIN   I am / not out to sabotage the play.

LAN PING   Then why make Joan such a coward?

LI LIN   Dreams die. Friendships fail. But somehow she will break through to the other side of despair –

LAN PING   Yeah. She'll die.

LI LIN   On her own terms.

LAN PING   Dead is dead.

LI LIN   When you play Joan of Arc, make her whatever you want. Now get out.

LAN PING   I can't go out there! Li Lin! I can't! I'd rather kill
            myself.

LI LIN   (*Cold*.) Stop being such a drama queen.

LAN PING   Tang Na jumped into the river this morning. I
            never expected he'd actually – What do you think
            his friends will do, to this slut who drove him to –
            I wanted to shout to you while you were on stage
            'Li Lin I'm here!' But *everyone* in this building is
            a friend of Tang Na's. If they knew I was here…

            Beat.

LI LIN   The next scene is a big group scene. Everyone
            will be on stage. Let yourself out then.

            LI LIN *heads for the door.*

LAN PING   (*Blocking her*.) I said I was sorry! You want me to
            grovel?

            Beat.

            'If we shadows have offended,
            Think but this, and all is mended'

            LI LIN *snorts.*

            Please, Li Lin. You're so good at detecting
            emotional undercurrents… Please.

            Pause.

            I shouldn't have abandoned you. I'm sorry.

            Long pause.

LI LIN   Where are you staying?

LAN PING   At the Peace Hotel.

LI LIN   What??

LAN PING   Eat drink and be merry for tomorrow we die!

LI LIN   (*Firmly*.) No one's dying tomorrow.
            Tang Na didn't die. He was pulled out of the
            river. It's all in the tabloids.

            Beat.

LAN PING   (*Deflated.*) I bet they're still braying for my blood.

MAN   (*Offstage.*) Five minutes, Li Lin, five minutes until you're on.

LI LIN   Shanghai's not safe. You can't stay here. There'll be a military convoy for Yan'an. We're expecting it any day.

LAN PING   Well, I can't go.

LI LIN   But you're a Party member.

LAN PING   Tang Na's resurrected the old rumour.

LI LIN   What rumour?

LAN PING   (*Slowly.*) You know I told you I was arrested for doing street theatre? I got out after three months. Much sooner than all the others… They thought I must have confessed to get out. But I hadn't! I sang arias to cheer myself up and the guards liked it, so they released me… (*Pleadingly.*) I didn't denounce anyone…

        Pause

LI LIN   Anyone can break in jail. Even a Joan of Arc.

LAN PING   They won't let me on that convoy.

LI LIN   You'll get on that convoy. I'll vouch for you.

LAN PING   Thanks but no thanks.

LI LIN   Lan Ping! The Japanese army is twenty miles away –

LAN PING   I found fame in Shanghai. I found my vocation in Shanghai. I found a home… I'm going down with Shanghai.

LI LIN   (*Fiercely.*) You've always accused the Party of not taking art seriously. Well here's your chance. Come to Yan'an. Make your case to Chairman Mao. Tell him that culture is revolution.

MAN   (*Offstage.*) Li Lin. Now.

             LI LIN *fastens the helmet of her armour.*

LI LIN   Wait. For. Me.

             LI LIN *turns towards the audience and steps into the spotlight. She bows. Thunderous applause.*

             LAN PING *jealously stalks her with her eyes.*

News

'Shanghai Times, *September 1937: Japanese Troops Invade Shanghai.*'

'South China Morning Post, *November, 1937: Japanese Troops Take Shanghai.*'

'Red China, *December 1937: Japanese Troops Invade the Capital City of Nanking, and Massacre 40,000 Civilians.*'

Scene Four

Title: 'Xian, 1938.'

Dawn.

A school, repurposed to house refugees waiting to be vetted. A large portrait of Mao Zedong presides over the space.

LAN PING *is sleeping on a bench. She uses her bag as a pillow.*

LI LIN *enters.*

LI LIN   Lan Ping!

> LI LIN *gently shakes* LAN PING *awake.* LAN PING *startles, sits up, clutches her bag with one hand and wards off* LI LIN *with the other.*

LAN PING   What? Thief! Get off me!

LI LIN   It's me, Li Lin.

LAN PING   (*Now fully awake.*) Li Lin?
Where did you go? I was so worried –

LI LIN   We need to go now.

LAN PING   Where?

LI LIN   Yan'an.

LAN PING   Just like that? Without a pass? There's thousands of people ahead of us; we haven't even been processed yet –

LI LIN   I'll tell you on the way.

LAN PING   I can't go there. They've just brought up that whole Tang Na libel that I confessed instead of being shot. But my luck's turned. I ran into an old acquaintance yesterday. (*With a flourish.*) Kang Sheng.

LI LIN   Chairman Mao's Head of Secret Service?

LAN PING   Yep.

LI LIN   (*Disbelieving.*) How do you know him?

> *Beat.*

LAN PING   My mother used to work for his family. He promised to erase the – irregularities – in my file and get us passes to Yan'an!   (*Defensively.*) Yes. For a price.

LI LIN   Lan Ping, there's no need for you to turn to the likes of Kang Sheng –

> *Screaming and indistinct shouting from outside.*

LAN PING   What was that?

LI LIN   Nothing.

LAN PING   *Who* was that? You know something.

LI LIN   That's Comrade He. Chairman Mao's wife.
                (*Softly.*) She has twenty shrapnel wounds from
                the Long March. She's being sent for treatment to
                Moscow.

                *More shouting. Sound of blows, and the thudding
                sound of someone being dragged along the floor.*

                She's suffered mentally too...

LAN PING   (*Stares.*) What a loon.

LI LIN   (*Indignantly.*) Comrade He is a woman warrior;
                a comrade-in-arms to Chairman Mao –

LAN PING   And Mao has grown tired of every single one of
                those wounds.

LI LIN   Lan Ping!

LAN PING   They're literally dragging her by her hair.
                Obviously Mao doesn't give a shit. Who's the
                other woman?

LI LIN   What other woman?

LAN PING   She was shouting about Mao and some Shanghai
                hussy.

LI LIN   (*Firmly.*) We don't have time for gossip –

LAN PING   (*Musingly.*) There must be ten men for every
                woman here, and most of the women are so...
                leathery.

LI LIN   Lan Ping! You're not –

LAN PING   (*Tossing her hair.*) Of course not. We're not
                concubines hustling for the emperor's favour.
                (*Beat.*) I wish I knew how else to break through
                though.

                The sound of Jeeps revving up.

LI LIN	We're leaving. Now.
LAN PING	What?
LI LIN	Here's your pass to Yan'an.
LAN PING	*How?* This is a military pass.
LI LIN	Please. I don't have time to explain –
LAN PING	Li Lin. What's going on?
LI LIN	(*Deep breath.*) I'm not actually Li Lin.
LAN PING	What do you mean?
LI LIN	My real name is Sun Weishi. My father Sun Bingwen was shot by the Nationalists. We all had to take on new names and go into hiding.
LAN PING	Sun Bingwen. The military director? (*Slowly.*) So your 'Papa Zhou' is Zhou Enlai. The Vice Chairman of the Party. Mao's number two.
LI LIN	Yes.
LAN PING	You lied to me.
LI LIN	I used a pseudonym –
LAN PING	I thought you were a half-orphan, abandoned by her mother; but all the time you were actually a red princess; Communist royalty – everything between us is fake!
LI LIN	You don't use *your* real name –
LAN PING	Poor little Li Lin… who is actually Sun Weishi – Sun 'Sustainer of the World'. Your parents had lofty goals for you. It all makes sense now. Of course you are a red princess. You move through the world as if you *belong*…
LI LIN	The secret police were hunting us. I swore never to reveal my real name to anyone –
LAN PING	I'm not *anyone*.

LI LIN   Lan Ping, please… I could have endangered you!
              My father was shot –

LAN PING   And my mother was nearly beaten to death. See
              this tooth? My father was beating my mother
              with a metal spade. I tried to stop him. His
              spade knocked my tooth loose. We fled my
              father's house that night. She hired herself out
              as a bedwarmer for rich children, warming their
              feet on her belly while they slept; warming the
              beds of their father – there it is again, that flicker
              of disgust – yes she 'sold herself'. She had no
              choice. Will her name ever enter the history
              books? Whereas your father is enshrined in the
              Communist pantheon. Is that fair?

LI LIN   In the new China, women will be honoured.

LAN PING   Bullshit. Look at this place. Crawling with
              desperate refugees. Getting into Yan'an depends
              on having a male patron. You've nabbed one of
              the greatest – Vice Chairman Zhou Enlai.

LI LIN   He signed your pass.

LAN PING   And I should be grateful? If I wanted to go to
              Yan'an, I'll get in. If not through the front gate,
              I'll find the side door. Kang Sheng will deliver.

LI LIN   Kang Sheng's a Krogstad. He'll demand a pound
              of flesh for any favour, then stab you in the back.

LAN PING   We know each other very well. My mother used
              to warm his feet as a child. I'll remind him of
              a few little facts.

LI LIN   You would rather be indebted to a man like Kang
              Sheng than accept my help?

LAN PING   Kang Sheng and I understand each other.

LI LIN   Lan Ping. Whatever you think of me. This is
              a military pass. To travel to Yan'an on those Jeeps
              outside. These are the only military vehicles

within two hundred miles. Everything else has
been deployed to the front lines in Wuhan. You
don't have to share a Jeep with me. You don't
ever have to speak to me again. But you do have
to come. Now.

LAN PING   Li Shumeng.

LI LIN   What?

LAN PING   My birth name.

LI LIN   That's very... sweet.

LAN PING   Is it? Li 'gentle and dim-witted'. And you are Sun
'Sustainer of the World'. That's the difference
between us. You were wanted. Your parents
saw the potential in you. My father whipped my
mother. For giving birth to a girl.

MAN   (*Offstage.*) Comrade Sun. We're leaving now.

The sound of Jeeps starting to drive off.

LAN PING   (*With finality.*) Goodbye, Sun Weishi.

SUN *leaves.*

LAN PING *thinks. She belts in her military
fatigues to show off her perfect waist. She
lets down her long hair, running her fingers
luxuriously through the strands. She ties her
kerchief jauntily under her chin, accentuating her
features. She looks around cautiously to make
sure no one is watching. She retrieves a locket of
rouge powder on a necklace concealed under her
uniform.*

*She applies rouge to her cheeks, and dabs some
on her lips.*

This Shanghai hussy is ready for battle.

*The 'Dance of the Knights' from Prokofiev's
Romeo and Juliet plays in her head. The portrait*

*of Mao lights up. LAN PING fixes her eyes on
the portrait and dances slowly, menacingly, but
also sensually, in an eerie resemblance to the
proletariat ballets for which she is later famous.*

Big Character Posters (1939)

*Projections of posters with large handwritten Chinese
characters and caricatures.*

*'Down with the Shanghai slut!' next to a caricature of Lan Ping
in a military cap and high heels.*

*'Save Chairman Mao from the Poisoned Apple!' alongside
a picture of a blue apple.*

*'Japanese Rejoice as Vixen Distracts Mao from War!' next to
a caricature of Lan Ping swathed in fox furs straddling Mao in
bed.*

Scene Five

Titles: 'Yan'an, 1939.'

*A barn dance in Yan'an: packed mud floor, lit cheaply by
coloured paper lanterns.*

*Music: jazz, played by a motley collection of instruments
(An erhu, a zither, a trombone – whatever instruments were
available in war time.)*

SUN enters tentatively.

JIANG   You weren't invited.

SUN   I know you never want to see me again…

JIANG   —

SUN   I should have followed the logic of the heart and told you my real name, Party discipline be – I'm sorry, Lan Ping.

JIANG   Jiang Qing.

SUN   What?

JIANG   You're not the only one with a shiny new name.

SUN   A new name?

JIANG   Jiang Qing. 'Bright blue river.' What do you think, Sun Weishi Sustainer of the World?

SUN   It is a... bold name.

JIANG   It is a wonderful name. From now on I shall no longer be a blue apple, a freak of nature, but a river that surges into the ocean. The river sustains; the river destroys. This name is a gift from Chairman Mao; a message from Chairman Mao to the world –

SUN   He renamed you?

JIANG   Don't be so judgy! He adores me. (*Airily.*) We've got a three-bedroom cave! Even Zhou Enlai only has two. When we take Beijing, we'll move to the imperial palace!

SUN   (*Repelled.*) Sounds like you have it all figured out.

JIANG   I'm taking over the theatre that the Empress Dowager built.

    Jazz music strikes up.

    Jitterbug time! Where's Zhou Enlai?

    Beat.

SUN   Papa Zhou's getting ready for his trip to Moscow tomorrow.

JIANG   (*Pouts.*) He's the only man who can dance in Yan'an. Never mind. You'll do.

          JIANG *seizes hold of* SUN. *She dances wildly.*

SUN   I can't keep up!

JIANG   You'll have to. I only feel free on the dance floor.

SUN   You don't sound happy?

JIANG   Are you? Has Yan'an lived up to your expectations of a socialist utopia? Huh?

SUN   (*Cautiously.*) We are in a transitional phase –

JIANG   This place is an open-air prison... I can't breathe. But everything will change once I get married.

SUN   But you're against marriage.

JIANG   (*Releasing* SUN *violently.*) You've joined them to sabotage my engagement?

SUN   You're still my friend! I want you to be happy! Will marrying Chairman Mao make you... happy?

          JIANG *is silent.*

          (*With consternation.*) The Chairman's coming this way!

JIANG   Don't worry. Kang Sheng is under strict orders to keep Mao supplied with dancing partners. Look at the silly grin on that little nurse's face.

SUN   Aren't you jealous?

JIANG   I have no desire to dance the train-track dance.

SUN   The what?

JIANG   I'll show you.

          JIANG *pushes* SUN *in a vertical line towards the back of the stage while mechanically stepping in time to the music.*

All change!

JIANG turns SUN around ninety degrees and pushes her in a straight line towards the wings, stepping on her toes.

All change!

JIANG changes direction again and pushes SUN along.

SUN   (*Laughing.*) Okay okay I get the idea! (*Sideways glance at Mao.*) You shouldn't make it so obvious –

JIANG   Imitation is the sincerest form of flattery.

JIANG flashes a melting smile at the (invisible) Mao.

(*Whispers.*) He's confusing a dance with a tank manoeuvre.

They both laugh. The dancing gets wilder.

Much better. You're finally swinging your hips. Your Papa Zhou can really swing his. (*Beat.*) I heard he legally adopted you.

SUN   It was Mama Zhou's idea.

JIANG   Clever woman. Never underestimate the plain dumpy ones. By adopting you as their daughter, she's neutralised you as a rival...

SUN   That's... that's...

SUN breaks away from JIANG. JIANG catches hold of her and dips her hard.

JIANG   Wise up, Comrade Sun. Nest of vipers here. You're brilliant, beautiful, spirited, free... They stamp women into cogs here; for their killing machine. Every single wife here wants me dead.

SUN   No they don't. (*Beat.*) But Comrade He isn't

just the Chairman's wife, she's their comrade-in-arms –

JIANG   Mao sent her off to a Moscow asylum long before he met me!

SUN   They didn't have to come to your dance. They've turned up.

JIANG   Fabulous turnout. They come on Saturday to my dance. Then on Monday they scheme to bring me down. Did you see the school strike?

SUN *nods silently*

(*Quietly.*) I've been called many things… But somehow seeing kids, with their smooth round faces, calling for the death of the 'Shanghai actress' distracting Chairman Mao from the war and letting Japan conquer China… (*Even quieter.*) I felt like the scum of the earth.

SUN   Oh, Lan – Comrade Jiang… it's that old old stereotype of femme fatale actresses… But things are changing. Even Mummy! Papa Zhou worked on her, and she's agreed that I can study directing. I'm going to be a director!

JIANG   (*Wistfully.*) Everything comes up roses for you. (*Beat.*) They've started a political review against me.

SUN   I thought your fixer Kang Sheng took care of –

JIANG   I thought so too. (*Beat.*) He's not my fixer. He's Mao's fixer. He's hedging his bets. If I become Madam Mao – great. But if I fail, then he's got deniability. (*Abruptly.*) Has anyone asked you about posters?

SUN   What posters?

JIANG   Those Coca-Cola posters. Did you keep any?

SUN   I left Shanghai in such a rush –

JIANG   Someone. Somewhere. Has posters. Photos. My diary! Shanghai was a different world! Things that were fine there look different here. (*Softer.*) I've always been heart and soul a revolutionary.

SUN   I know…

JIANG   I'm so utterly alone.

SUN   But the Chairman loves you… and you love him?

Here the jazz music could turn into something more like Tchaikovsky, and the dancing slow to something more balletic, expressionistic.

Beat.

JIANG   There's something in me that thrills to him. Mao's an arsonist. It takes one to know one.

SUN   Would you love him even if he wasn't the Chairman?

JIANG   But he *is* the Chairman. What have you heard? Who's been scheming against him?

SUN   Nothing! Nobody! I just need to know… that your marriage will be a true communion.

JIANG   (*Slowly.*) The others on the Politburo. They all come from money. They've studied in Paris… But Mao and I. We're peasant trash. Hardscrabble weeds. We'll never have Paris.

SUN   But when you're together… do you feel that – glory, that heart expanding, that being at one –

JIANG   The thing you have to know about sex: it's engaging at the beginning. But only power sustains interest in the long run. And I want the power to say fuck you to the Politburo. Can you keep a secret?

SUN   I've kept all your secrets.

JIANG   Mao's telegraphed Stalin to approve our

marriage. I'd like to know which one of them would still have the balls to oppose me, once we have Stalin's blessing.

JIANG *executes a triumphant stampede of a dance move.* SUN *breaks away.*

What is it?

SUN   —

JIANG   Something's happened. Did Stalin reply?

SUN   —

JIANG   Zhou Enlai knows something.

SUN   Papa Zhou would never break Party discipline –

JIANG   You suspect something.

SUN   —

JIANG   Still the obedient revolutionary?

               Pause.

SUN   The Politburo came today to Papa Zhou's cave.

JIANG   They're plotting against Mao –

SUN   The Chairman came too.

JIANG   (*Slowly.*) So this is about me.

SUN   I was in Papa Zhou's study, in the little nook at the back where he keeps his novels. I heard them coming in. I didn't dare come out because Papa Zhou doesn't like people knowing – Anyway. All I heard was Chairman Mao saying that Stalin agrees. And something about a disclaimer.

JIANG   What disclaimer?

               Pause.

SUN   That you are not to enter politics for thirty years.

Beat.

JIANG   And what did Mao say?

SUN   That you'd sign.

Long pause.

The music stops.

JIANG   So it comes to this. I alone of all the wives must sign a disclaimer. Because they are virtuous revolutionaries and I a gold-digging power-hungry slut.

SUN   No!

JIANG   I married an art critic! For love. (*Softly.*) Tang Na broke my heart.

SUN   I know.

JIANG   Thirty years… they want to bury me alive… I'm an artist! I need freedom like a fish needs water!

SUN   Come with me to Moscow. Tomorrow.

JIANG   Tomorrow?

SUN   I'm flying out with Papa Zhou. I'm going to study at Stanislavski's Moscow Art Theatre. 'To Moscow to Moscow, to Moscow, now.'

JIANG   (*Coldly.*) You have a powerful patron who supports you without demanding to fuck you. Do you think Mao is the least bit interested in my artistic growth?

SUN   How could the Chairman possibly deny your request to study in Moscow?

Beat.

JIANG   I'm pregnant.

SUN   Congratulations!

JIANG   For getting knocked up where I can't get an

abortion? Stick a woman in fatigues, put a wrench in her hand, an axe, a machine gun – they're just props, unless she can live her life freely – take lovers, have abortions, make art not babies! Women hold up half of heaven? Only if they behave!

SUN   Come with me. I'll help with the baby.

JIANG   Do you think the mother of Chairman Mao's child would be allowed to live her own free life? Maybe I'd end up sharing an asylum cell with Comrade He. 'I must make up my mind who is right.' *I'm right.* I've got to get out. The door, where's the door?

JIANG starts banging on all the doors. SUN *tries to restrain her but* JIANG *is too strong.*

Jazz music. SUN *is suddenly conscious of everyone's eyes on them. She joins in with* JIANG *battering the doors, trying to make it look like a light-hearted dance move.*

JIANG gradually calms down. The dance morphs into a waltz with the two friends holding each other closely.

Can't you at least wait till after my wedding?

SUN   If I don't get on that military plane, I might not get another chance.

JIANG   To Moscow to Moscow... but it's just one sister who gets to go.

SUN   I'll write.

JIANG   Good. Cut down everything that stands in your path. My little Li Lin has grown up. You work hard for me. You become the best Goddamn director. Thirty years is not forever. One day we'll do *A Doll's House* together.

News

'South China Morning Post, *15 August 1945: Japan Surrenders Unconditionally.*'

'South China Morning Post, *1 October 1945: Civil War Breaks Out Between the Communists and the Nationalists.*'

'People's Daily, *1 October 1949: Chairman Mao Proclaims the New People's Republic of China from Tiananmen Gate.*'

'People's Daily, *December 1949: Chairman Mao Sets Off On His First State Visit to the USSR.*'

Scene Six

Titles: 'Beijing, 1950.'

An empty theatre.

JIANG enters. She plants herself centre-stage.

JIANG　　'I must make up my mind who is right – the world or I'

Gales of laughter from a neighbouring room. A group sings a folk song.

'I have been greatly wronged, Torvald. It is your fault that I have made nothing of my life.' (*Louder.*) 'I have made nothing of my life.' (*Screaming.*) 'I have made nothing of my life.'

The sounds cease from the next room.

SUN　　(*Offstage.*) From the top.

The singing resumes.

Sound of running footsteps.

SUN *bursts into the theatre.*

Comrade Jiang!

JIANG   Madam Artistic Director.

They run towards each other. A long hug.

Look at this. Didn't I tell you? The first female theatre director in China.

She caresses SUN*'s face.*

Ten years... it's been ten years.

SUN   I know... Papa Zhou said he hand-delivered my letters to you. Why didn't you ever write back?

JIANG   About what? That I was confined to Mao's kitchen, while you were conquering new plays, new worlds, new men? Do you know what it means to be kept out of politics when *everything* is political?

SUN   But I saw a photo of you and the Chairman on the frontline, riding on one horse. You were magnificent –

JIANG   I was. Jiang Qing enters the world historical stage!

SUN   So why did you leave for Moscow right after we won the war?

JIANG   You're not the only one who gets to go to Moscow. (*Beat.*) They put me right back in the doll's house. They wouldn't even let me join Mao for his victory lap at Tiananmen Square; didn't let me step foot on Tiananmen Gate when he proclaimed the founding of the new China. What choice did I have except to leave the country; escape humiliation?

JIANG*'s voice has risen. The singing next door falters.*

SUN   (*Softly, steering* JIANG.) I didn't know it was that
           bad. Shall we go somewhere more private?

JIANG   (*Pleadingly.*) I'm not leaving the stage. Everyone
           else is buzzing with new plays, new films, new
           projects. I'm the only one who has nothing!
           I came back yesterday from Moscow and went
           straight to the Culture Minister: 'I'm an artist, put
           me to work!' 'Comrade Jiang Qing, your most
           important revolutionary task is to look after the
           health of Chairman Mao.'

SUN   Come work with me! I'm sure I can sort
           something out with Papa Zhou. We'll just have
           to find you the right role; I've already announced
           my first season but –

JIANG   A series of dog-farts.

SUN   What?

JIANG   Your first season. Toothless. Tear it up. Put on
           A Doll's House. If you're too scared, let me do
           it. I'll be your Chairwoman. And your Executive
           Director. In fact I could be your Artistic Director
           and you focus on directing.

SUN   You can't just come and take over my theatre!

JIANG   You owe me.

SUN   I owe you?

JIANG   I've heard that my husband promised to build
           a National Theatre for you. What happened to
           inspire such generosity? We're at war with South
           Korea, *and* we're building you a new theatre?

SUN   You used to believe that theatre is the crucible of
           revolution.

JIANG   And how did you convince my husband that
           theatre is the crucible of revolution? (*Beat.*) What
           happened on your trip with Mao?

SUN   I was an official interpreter on a state visit to
        Moscow. I am not at liberty to disclose –

JIANG   Oh it's to be like that? Go ahead. Rub it in. You
        were the one who was chosen.

SUN   I didn't choose to go.

        Beat.

JIANG   I'm not blaming you for what happened.

SUN   (*Formal.*) Comrade Jiang Qing. I have no idea
        what you're talking about.

JIANG   A little bird told me that my husband called you
        in to his private train car 'to educate him on
        Russian language and culture'.

SUN   Comrade Jiang, you know Kang Sheng is not to
        be trusted –

JIANG   And that you later ran out in tears. Your dress
        torn –

SUN   Kang Sheng wants to turn you against me. To get
        at Papa Zhou. I just got engaged to Jin Shan! I am
        not your rival.

JIANG   You think I'm jealous of you? You think you're
        the first woman Mao's forced? Mind you most
        times he goes for little secretaries, nurses,
        dancers, not red princesses – and they're ever
        so honoured to be fucked by the Chairman
        himself. At least get checked out for syphilis. You
        wouldn't want to infect Jin Shan on your wedding
        night, would you?

SUN   I thought you'd be happy for me...

JIANG   A man who fucks everything that moves. Jin Shan
        will break your heart.

SUN   He's been really straight with me. I know you had
        a fling with him –

JIANG *swiftly pinions* SUN *against a wall*
(*maybe even presses her neck*).

JIANG   Never. Use. My. Past. Against. Me.

SUN   (*Afraid.*) No no no you inspired me – free love –

JIANG *releases her.*

Pause.

JIANG   (*Cold.*) How can you be bought so cheaply? How
could you sell your silence for a new theatre
building, an artistic directorship –

SUN   Within this theatre, I can offer my artists freedom.

JIANG   You really think Party logic stops at the gates
of your theatre? Do you know why my husband
broke his streak of disposable little women to
rape a red princess? He needed to prove that
his dick is bigger than Zhou Enlai's: I can rape
Zhou's adopted daughter and he'll just have to
swallow it. That's Party logic for you. Where's
your outrage? I heard you ran, sobbing, your
dress torn, to Zhou Enlai, *and he told you not to
make a fuss.* 'Think of the Party.' He should have
sent you right back on the next train. Can't you
see? To my husband, to Zhou Enlai, to Jin Shan.
We are just a series of holes, to be fucked at will,
then thrown away. When I played Nora, women
cast off their shackles! Doors slammed across
Shanghai! Across China! We can do it again. Call
out the patriarchy, the rapists, the men, the men,
the men who keep us down. Burn down the doll's
house! Burn it all down!

By now, JIANG *is shouting.*

The singing has ceased.

Pause.

SUN   (*Controlled.*) Nothing happened.

News

'People's Daily, *1958: Chairman Mao launches programme of Total Industrialisation for a Great Leap Forward into the Future!'*

'South China Morning Post, *1959: Rumours of Catastrophic Famine Sweeping China.'*

'South China Morning Post, *1962: 20 Million Famine Deaths Spur 'Reformist clique' to Challenge Mao.'*

The whole stage is flooded with red light.

'People's Daily, *1966: Comrade Jiang Qing, Key Architect of Cultural Revolution, Pledges to Crush Counterrevolutionary Forces.'*

Scene Seven

Titles: 'Beijing, 1966.'

A villa. JIANG *is in a fur coat.*

SUN *enters, dressed in a padded cottonwool jacket with the stuffing coming out at the seams.*

SUN	Comrade Jiang! We have nothing, nothing, nothing from the past. They've taken away our letters, our photos, my directing notes –
JIANG	What are you talking about?
SUN	The Red Guards came to our house then they struggled against Jin Shan and shaved his head. Please, Comrade Jiang –
JIANG	Can we – just for tonight – be Li Lin and Lan Ping?

SUN   Lan Ping. Please! I just want to reassure you – we have nothing. No letters, no postcards, no posters of you. We destroyed everything a long time ago. There are no traces of your past.

JIANG   (*Slowly*.) You've erased me.

SUN   Not from my memory! I would never betray you.

JIANG   That's why I need you, Li Lin. You remember me before I became Jiang Qing.

SUN   Yes yes and I am begging Lan Ping now, if you cherish our friendship... please tell your Red Guards that Jin Shan is not a counter-revolutionary.

JIANG   Oh, Li Lin. I would love to help. But just think. My beautiful Red Guards – they're sixteen... seventeen... you remember that age, all fire and flame – passionate Joan of Arcs, all two million of them – They saw those decadent film posters of Jin Shan. What did you expect?

SUN   Please! I totally understand why you're settling scores with the old Shanghai crowd.

JIANG   Is that what you think I'm doing? Settling old scores?

        Revenge is sweet... But it's bigger than that. We need to smash the old ways, crush the Cultural Establishment.

SUN   Jin Shan's no longer part of the Cultural Establishment –

JIANG   But you are. You've been avoiding me for the last fifteen years.

SUN   That's not true –

JIANG   Five times I've come to you with new projects. You fobbed me off. Why?

SUN   I don't remember – probably budget… timing…

JIANG   I'll tell you why. You've joined the Cultural Establishment… against me.

SUN   No! I've been living out in the oil fields, creating theatre with the oil workers –

JIANG   Proletarian dress-up.

SUN   We're finally creating a revolutionary theatre. Theatre for the people, co-created with the people; theatre with artistic rigour – new forms for new stories –

JIANG   And that's precisely why I want you at my side. The thirty years are drawing to a close. I am unchained. When everyone turned against my husband, he finally saw what I had known from the start. There's something rotten in the state of the Party. I'm the only one he can trust. We must appeal directly to the masses. That's why he asked me to start a Cultural Revolution. The whole resources of the state are behind me. Sky's the limit, Li Lin!
I am commissioning new works. Everything must be red, bright and shining. The heroes must be tall, mighty and wholesome. I shall ban everything else from our stages. I want to take your play and make it a musical.

SUN   You mean *The Sun Rises*?

JIANG   Yes! I've become obsessed with Rodgers and Hammerstein musicals. Have you watched *Oklahoma!*?

SUN   (*Wryly.*) We don't have access to banned western films.

                'Oh, What a Beautiful Morning' from Oklahoma! *starts playing in the background.*

JIANG   The curtains rise. Acres of shimmering oil fields.

A bright golden haze. Rigs reaching up to the sky… Then a hundred female oil workers shimmy down the rigs.
Of course many of your characters have to be eliminated or reformed.

SUN   (*Outraged.*) What?

JIANG   Especially the old women. We need revolutionary plays charged with positive energy –

SUN   But the older women carry the play!

JIANG   They are too bitter.

SUN   They lived through the famine –

JIANG   You are playing into Zhou Enlai's hands. He blames the famine on the Chairman.

             He tried to reverse the Chairman's policies –

SUN   – to make sure that another twenty million people don't starve.
             I heard about cannibalism.

             Beat.

JIANG   And you wove all that into the emotional undercurrent of your play. Counter-revolutionary, Comrade Sun.

SUN   I know it's not possible to tell stories like that now. But I have heard them and I cannot forget them and one day these stories *will* burst forth and there *will* be a reckoning.

             JIANG *takes out a photo of Zhou Enlai with the cast of the* Rising Sun.

             That's my photo! Your Red Guards seized it –

JIANG   When I saw Zhou Enlai posing with your oil worker 'actors', I finally understood. Zhou Enlai wants to create an alternative Cultural Revolution. To topple Mao. Do you know that this very morning he sent soldiers to stop my Red Guards from burning down the Forbidden City?

SUN   But why do you even want to burn down the Forbidden City?

JIANG   Because I can.

Beat

Zhou cannot stop my Cultural Revolution. I've swept away all the Old Guard artists and intellectuals. I've assembled an army of choreographers, composers and writers. All I need is the right director. Isn't it time you came over to my side? I want *The Sun Rises*.

SUN   It's not mine to give you.

JIANG   So it's a no?

SUN   The play belongs to the women oil workers. This is their truth.

JIANG   I define the truth. And I shall succeed. I have a good feeling about that.

JIANG sings the chorus from 'Oh, What a Beautiful Mornin' by Rodgers and Hammerstein. This segues straight to Jiang's photos of her model revolutionary works, ending with a photo of a woman shackled.

Scene Eight

Titles: 'Beijing, 1968.'

A prison. SUN is shackled. She is bleeding and bruised all over, and is on the point of death. She softly hums broken fragments from the folk song in Scene Six.

JIANG *enters and stands behind* SUN. *She observes* SUN *for a while, her face unreadable. Then she deliberately makes a noise.* SUN *realises someone is there.*

SUN	(*Weakly.*) Long live the revolution! Down with the traitors!
JIANG	Are you referring to me?
SUN	I am referring to Jiang Qing.
	SUN *tries to turn around.* JIANG *enters her field of vision.*
JIANG	(*Solicitously.*) How are you?
SUN	(*Laughs incredulously*.) I've been better.
JIANG	(*Genuine.*) I am sorry to hear that.
SUN	Are you? Lan Ping?
JIANG	There's no greater act of friendship than to expose the life-lie of a friend. That's why I've shut you up here.
SUN	Then let me be a friend to you. I think back on your life and it seems to me that you slammed the door on one doll's house, only to end up in a larger one with a crueller Torvald – your father, your grandfather, Tang Na… and now Mao. The ultimate Torvald.
	Pause. This has hit home.
JIANG	I forgot how much I enjoy talking to you. I'm remembering all the reasons why we are friends.
SUN	My other friends don't arrest and torture me.
JIANG	It's an unusual friendship. With you I always feel seen. (*Beat.*) I am using Mao as a battering ram.
SUN	There'll just be another doll house.
JIANG	Who can contain me now?

SUN   Listen to me, Lan Ping. Mao is dying. You have
                no independent power base. You start fires, but
                you can't put them out. Your chief ally is Kang
                Sheng, who will turn as soon as the tides of
                power shift. And most of all, Mao doesn't trust
                you. You're only his attack dog. He tells you who
                to bite – and you bite!

JIANG   Sun Weishi, you really are weary of life.

SUN   Jiang Qing, I have nothing more to lose.

JIANG   Who do you think you are? Joan of Arc? Dying
                on your own terms, canonised after death? Even
                your name will be ashes. And I shall be Mao's
                successor.

SUN   Mao's disbanded your Red Guards. He'll never
                name you his successor. He trusts Papa Zhou.

JIANG   Papa Zhou Papa Zhou Papa Zhou. Your Papa
                Zhou has thrown you under the bus!

SUN   I'm sure he's searching for me. Why else would
                you hide me here? This isn't a regular prison.
                This is a black site… torture is forbidden by the
                constitution!

JIANG   Is that what you've been telling yourself? And
                here I was thinking you must have superhuman
                endurance, in this black hole where most people
                lose their minds – their lives – within what? Two
                months tops? You've made it to seven.

SUN   Seven months, twelve days, five hours.

JIANG   (*Taken aback.*) People lose all sense of time here.

SUN   I hear the Bell Tower.

JIANG   You have gone mad after all. My Red Guards
                have ripped down the bells.

SUN   Today is the fourteenth of October 1968.

                Beat.

JIANG	Impressive. Which makes tomorrow your eighteenth wedding anniversary. Don't you want to spend it with Jin Shan?
SUN	(*Incredulous, electrified.*) Is he alive?
JIANG	He's fine.
SUN	But how – how can he – you took him away first.
JIANG	(*Soothing.*) He's in a regular prison. With proper rations, and daily exercise in the yard. We're not barbarians. He can tell you himself, tomorrow, if…
SUN	What's your price?
JIANG	Denounce Zhou Enlai as a spy and a traitor. Confess how Khrushchev turned him during your trip to Moscow.
SUN	That's ridiculous! Even your Kang Sheng has not found a shred of evidence –
JIANG	Your confession will be the evidence.
SUN	Not that. Please.
JIANG	It's your husband or Zhou Enlai.
SUN	What has Zhou Enlai ever done to you except be kind? When you were in Moscow for treatment, Mao never visited. Papa Zhou visited –
JIANG	(*Sneers.*) Saint Zhou the moderate. The compassionate. The urbane, cosmopolitan, voice of reason. Look who signed your arrest warrant. Zhou. En. Lai.
	JIANG *shows the warrant to* SUN, *who is shocked to the core.*
SUN	You must have forced him.
JIANG	Everyone has a choice.

SUN	H
JIANG	Help me.
SUN	Let us both go. Now. Without a confession. Lan Ping. You can choose to release us both. You've been swept out to sea by a raging river. 'The suffering sea is endless, but turn back, and there is the shore.' I am your shore. Come back, Lan Ping.

The sound of bells ringing.

JIANG	It's the fifteenth. Your anniversary. You could still walk free.
SUN	You hear the bells too?

JIANG picks up the confession and thrusts it at SUN.

JIANG	Why won't you come over to me?
SUN	Because I will not betray Lan Ping.
JIANG	We went to the theatre like it was a temple. Can't we do that again, like it's 1935?
SUN	For that the miracle of miracles must happen…
JIANG	What is the miracle of miracles?
SUN	Oh, Lan Ping. I don't believe any more…

SUN dies.

Blackout.

Titles:

'Sun Weishi (1921–1968).'

'September 1976: Mao Zedong dies.'

'October 1976: Jiang Qing is arrested for the murder of countless victims.'

'1982: Jiang Qing is sentenced to death, commuted to a life sentence, and is put to work making rag dolls.'

Historical footage: Lan Ping singing a love song in a 1930s Shanghai movie.

Coda

A rehearsal room.

The sound of an air siren.

Spotlight on LAN PING *who runs onto stage.*

LAN PING   (*Fretfully.*) Where are you, Li Lin? Li Lin! We've
            got to hide! (*Whimpers.*) I'm hungry. I'm cold.
            They can't keep on closing down the theatre.
            How are we going to eat?

            Lights up on LI LIN *and an enormous Christmas
            tree. Their shoes are lined up underneath the tree.*
            LAN PING *stares.*

LI LIN   It's okay. We're together. We'll be safe under
            the Christmas tree. Nothing can come between
            us. And who knows. Tomorrow morning our
            shoes might be filled with chocolate... and silver
            coins... and a nutcracker Prince...

            LI LIN *lies down.* LAN PING *joins her. Lights
            blaze on the Christmas tree.*

            Titles: '1991.'

            A prison filled with rag dolls.

            JIANG *unravels a few dolls and ties the cloth into
            a noose. She hangs up the noose from the ceiling.*

            Blackout.

            Title: 'Jiang Qing 1914–1991.'

Thanks

I'd like to thank Indhu Rubasingham for commissioning this play in the depths of the pandemic, when it felt as though theatre might never return, and for her decisive dramaturgical intervention after the first draft. The play is much stronger as a result.

My thanks also to Amit Sharma and Tom Wright for their dramaturgical support, and for believing in the piece and programming it – it's an honour to be part of Amit's first season.

Heartfelt thanks to my director, Katie Posner, for her kind, playful, and forensic approach throughout both the development and rehearsal process. It's been extraordinary to see the play come into focus under her care.

Finally, my deepest thanks to the cast, creatives, and company for bringing this play so vividly to life.

A.N.

So How Much of This Is True?
Amy Ng

It's the question I've been asked most often – from the conception of this play, through its long gestation, and now, at last, its appearance on stage. It's usually followed, once my interlocutor learns I used to be a historian, by a second: 'How do you justify fictionalising history?' Or, more generously: 'How is writing a historical play different from writing history?'

Let me begin with that last question before circling back to the first two. In both disciplines, you start with a question. Mine was this: how does a woman artist who once worshipped freedom, who fought to liberate women from patriarchal oppression, who believed that art was the royal road to freedom, become a lieutenant of a regime that silenced a generation of artists? How did the woman once synonymous with *A Doll's House* turn on other women? And what does this metamorphosis tell us about the society that shaped her? About the position of women? About the relationship between artists and power?

The next step, for both playwrights and historians, is to try to establish what actually happened. (I categorically reject the notion that fiction gives you licence to go against established historical facts. Facts are the warp and weft of the tapestry. Pull one thread, and the whole pattern begins to unravel.) But establishing the facts is easier said than done. Historical narratives are smooth. The evidence they rest on is not. History is famously written by the victors, and the victors curate the record – preserving what flatters them, erasing what does not.

Jiang Qing was no victor. Her papers, her legacy, the official story of her life, have been shaped not only by the Party that sentenced her to death, but by the victims who survived her. Even the basics remain cloudy. When did she arrive in Yan'an from Shanghai? When did she first meet Mao, and under what circumstances? Did Stalin personally broker a compromise between Mao and the rest of the Politburo to allow their marriage, as was widely rumoured?

Historians live in archives. We are trained to seek primary sources unfiltered by the interpretations of others. But the party archives that likely contain the most material on Jiang Qing remain sealed. Hence I turned to published primary sources: interviews she gave as an actress, articles she wrote on theatre and feminism scattered through various Shanghai newspapers in the 1930s, her speeches during the Cultural Revolution, transcripts of her trial, and newspaper clippings. I also read memoirs – mostly written by those who had been her victims. These are understandably polemical, and tend to see Jiang through the prism of her relationships with powerful men. But to understand how Jiang Qing, the woman artist, became the enforcer of patriarchal violence, I needed to place her in relation to other women. One name surfaced again and again: Sun Weishi – China's first female theatre director, and the adopted daughter of Premier Zhou Enlai.

Sun's historical traces are even more elusive than Jiang's. Jiang ensured that all Sun's papers were burned. Jiang had Sun cremated within hours of death to prevent an autopsy. Sun worked in theatre – that most perishable of art forms. Though she had been a prolific letter-writer, few letters survive. It is possible a trove of her letters remains in Zhou Enlai's sealed archives. But for now, the gaps have been filled with wildly speculative guesswork. In a society where official narratives were widely distrusted, a whole cottage industry of 'secret histories' – usually compilations of shocking, frequently salacious allegations against top leaders – sprang up. The explosive accusation that Jiang makes in Scene Six belongs to this category.

English-language sources on Sun are no more reliable. For instance, Ross Terrill, whose biography remains the most widely read English-language work on Jiang Qing, claims Sun was married twice and that she snatched away Jiang's lover in

Yan'an, thus incurring Jiang's enmity.[1] In fact, Sun was married only once, to the actor Jin Shan – Jiang's co-star in Shanghai, with whom she may or may not have had a fleeting affair. Terrill also misdates Sun's departure to Moscow by several years. Sun's entry in Wikipedia (as of March 2025) is riddled with errors, but given the scarcity of English-language material on Sun, it has become the only source on her life for many.

For this play, I have relied on memoirs and oral histories by Sun's friends, family, and fellow prisoners. What emerges from the evidence is that Sun was brilliant, generous, and greatly beloved; that her theatrical works were groundbreaking; that she succeeded in winning the deep trust and respect of colleagues and friends, despite the patriarchal bias against women leaders. Not surprisingly, then, Sun has often been cast as the saint, and Jiang as the villain consumed by jealousy.[2]

But what do we actually know of their relationship?

We know that Jiang Qing and Sun Weishi met in 1930s Shanghai, at the League of Left-Wing Dramatists. We are told they may have acted together – perhaps in Shanghai, perhaps later in Yan'an. We know that Jiang Qing attended Sun's wedding and brought extravagant gifts. We know that in the 1950s and '60s, Jiang sought Sun out repeatedly, proposing artistic collaborations, which Sun refused. And that in 1966, Sun told her sister: 'Jiang is coming after me. I know everything about her.' Finally, we know that Sun's death was cruel even by the standards of the Cultural Revolution. Jiang reportedly ordered that Sun be kept alive, but that she should be raped and tortured over months in a black site prison run by the Air Force, outside the regular legal system. We know that Jiang renamed her with a homonym of her real name – so instead of 'Weishi,' meaning 'Sustainer of the World,' Sun's prison name was 'Weishi' as in 'hypocrite.'

---

1   Ross Terrill, *Madame Mao: The White Boned Demon*, Simon and Schuster, 1992
2   Many of these are collected in China's National Theatre Ed., *An Innocent Heart: For the 91st Anniversary of the Birth of Sun Weishi (Wei You Chi Zi Xin)*. Beijing: Xinhua Publishing House, 2012

Had I written this as history, I would have hedged my hypotheses. Sun's assertion that she knew everything about Jiang's Shanghai days *suggests* a close friendship. *Perhaps* the cruelty of her death stemmed from something deeply personal – a perceived rejection, a felt betrayal. It is *plausible* Jiang saw her as a rival. Historians speak in conditionals. But conditionals are conjectures; a disguised form of fiction. Hence I turned to theatre – to make the empathetic leap and fill the void in the historical record.

This is the story of Sun Weishi and Jiang Qing: of how they became friends, of why the friendship failed – and of intimations of another world where they could have stayed friends and free artists.

Other Titles in this Series

Mike Bartlett
THE 47TH
ALBION
BULL
GAME
AN INTERVENTION
KING CHARLES III
MIKE BARTLETT PLAYS: TWO
MRS DELGADO
SCANDALTOWN
SNOWFLAKE
UNICORN
VASSA *after* Gorky
WILD

Sonali Bhattacharyya
CHASING HARES
KING TROLL (THE FAWN)
LIBERATION SQUARES
TWO BILLION BEATS

Jez Butterworth
THE FERRYMAN
THE HILLS OF CALIFORNIA
JERUSALEM
JEZ BUTTERWORTH PLAYS: ONE
JEZ BUTTERWORTH PLAYS: TWO
MOJO
THE NIGHT HERON
PARLOUR SONG
THE RIVER
THE WINTERLING

Mohamed-Zain Dada
BLUE MIST
DIZZY

Lucy Kirkwood
BEAUTY AND THE BEAST
  with Katie Mitchell
BLOODY WIMMIN
THE CHILDREN
CHIMERICA
HEDDA *after* Ibsen
THE HUMAN BODY
IT FELT EMPTY WHEN THE HEART
  WENT AT FIRST BUT IT IS
  ALRIGHT NOW
LUCY KIRKWOOD PLAYS: ONE
MOSQUITOES
NSFW
RAPTURE
TINDERBOX
THE WELKIN

Kimber Lee
UNTITLED F*CK M*SS S**GON PLAY

Young Jean Lee
STRAIGHT WHITE MEN
UNTITLED FEMINIST SHOW

Amy Ng
ACCEPTANCE
SHANGRI-LA

Azuka Oforka
THE WOMEN OF LLANRUMNEY

Suzan-Lori Parks
FATHER COMES HOME FROM THE WARS
  (PARTS 1, 2 & 3)
TOPDOG/UNDERDOG
WHITE NOISE

Sam Steiner
KANYE THE FIRS
LEMONS LEMONS LEMONS LEMONS
  LEMONS
A TABLE TENNIS PLAY
YOU STUPID DARKNESS!

Jack Thorne
2ND MAY 1997
AFTER LIFE *after* Hirokazu Kore-eda
BUNNY
BURYING YOUR BROTHER IN
  THE PAVEMENT
A CHRISTMAS CAROL *after* Dickens
THE END OF HISTORY...
HOPE
JACK THORNE PLAYS: ONE
JACK THORNE PLAYS: TWO
JUNKYARD
LET THE RIGHT ONE IN
  after John Ajvide Lindqvist
THE MOTIVE AND THE CUE
MYDIDAE
THE SOLID LIFE OF SUGAR WATER
STACY & FANNY AND FAGGO
WHEN WINSTON WENT TO WAR WITH
  THE WIRELESS
WHEN YOU CURE ME
WOYZECK *after* Büchner

debbie tucker green
BORN BAD
DEBBIE TUCKER GREEN PLAYS: ONE
DIRTY BUTTERFLY
EAR FOR EYE
HANG
NUT
A PROFOUNDLY AFFECTIONATE,
  PASSIONATE DEVOTION TO SOMEONE
  (– NOUN)
RANDOM
STONING MARY
TRADE & GENERATIONS
TRUTH AND RECONCILIATION

Tom Wells
BIG BIG SKY
BROKEN BISCUITS
DRIP *with* Matthew Robins
FOLK
JUMPERS FOR GOALPOSTS
THE KITCHEN SINK
ME, AS A PENGUIN
STUFF

Ross Willis
WOLFIE
WONDER BOY

A Nick Hern Book

Shanghai Dolls first published in Great Britain as a paperback original in 2025 by Nick Hern Books Limited, The Glasshouse, 49a Goldhawk Road, London W12 8QP in association with Kiln Theatre.

Shanghai Dolls copyright © 2025 Amy Ng

Amy Ng has asserted her right to be identified as the author of this work

Cover design by Muse Creative Communications

Designed and typeset by Nick Hern Books, London
Printed in Great Britain by Mimeo Ltd, Huntingdon, Cambridgeshire PE29 6XX

A CIP catalogue record for this book is available from the British Library

ISBN 978 1 83904 418 2

www.nickhernbooks.co.uk/environmental-policy

Nick Hern Books' authorised representative in the EU is
Easy Access System Europe – Mustamäe tee 50, 10621 Tallinn, Estonia
email gpsr.requests@easproject.com

www.nickhernbooks.co.uk

@nickhernbooks